JEWS AND THE
FOUNDING OF
THE REPUBLIC

JEWS AND THE FOUNDING OF THE REPUBLIC

Edited by:

Jonathan D. Sarna, Benny Kraut, Samuel K. Joseph

Sponsored by:

The Center for the Study of American Jewish Experience
Hebrew Union College-Jewish Institute of Religion, Cincinnati, Ohio

The International Center for University Teaching of Jewish Civilization
Jerusalem, Israel

 Markus Wiener Publishing

For information write to:
Markus Wiener Publishing, Inc.
2901 Broadway, New York, NY 10025

Cover design by Cheryl Mirkin

ISBN 0-910129-44-4

Library of Congress Card Catalog
Card No. 85-040513

Printed in the United States of America

Acknowledgement

The following publishers have generously given permission to reprint material from copyrighted works: From *Publications of the American Jewish Historical Society*, Volume 27, (c) 1920 by the American Jewish Historical Society. From Joseph L. Blau and Salo W. Baron (eds.), *The Jews of the United States, 1790-1840: A Documentary History*, (c) 1963 by Columbia University Press. From Conrad Cherry, *God's New Israel: Religious Interpretations of American Destiny*, (c) 1971 by Prentice Hall, Inc. From Stanley F. Chyet, *Lopez of Newport*, (c) 1970 by Wayne State University Press. From Jacob R. Marcus, *The American Colonial Jew: A Study in Acculturation*, (c) 1967 by Department of Religion, Syracuse University, by permission of Jacob R. Marcus. From Jacob R. Marcus (ed.), *Jews and the American Revolution: A Bicentennial Documentary*, (c) 1975 by the American Jewish Archives. From Jacob R. Marcus (ed.), *American Jewry Documents: Eighteenth Century*, (c) 1958 by the American Jewish Archives. From Gladys Rosen (ed.), *Jewish Life in America: Historical Perspectives*, (c) 1978 by the American Jewish Committee. From Jonathan D. Sarna, "The Impact of the American Revolution on the American Jew," (c) 1981 by Johns Hopkins University Press. From Oscar and Mary Handlin, "The Acquisition of Political and Social Rights by the Jews in the United States," (c) 1955 by the American Jewish Year Book. From Moshe Davis, *With Eyes Toward Zion*, (c) 1977 by Arno Press, by permission of Moshe Davis. From *The Bible in America: Essays in Cultural History*, (c) 1982 by Oxford University Press, by permission of Mark A. Noll. From Morris U. Schappes, *A Documentary History of the Jews in the United states*, (c) 1971 by Morris U. Schappes. From Edwin Wolf 2nd and Maxwell Whiteman, *The History of the Jews of Philadelphia*, (c) 1956 by the Jewish Publication Society of America. From E. James Ferguson, *The Papers of Robert Morris, Volume II*, (c) 1975 by the University of Pittsburgh Press. From Herbert J. Storing, *The Complete Anti-Federalist*, Volume IV, (c) 1981 by the University of Chicago Press.

CONTENTS

PREFACE

This volume was first conceived at a meeting called to discuss "Teaching the American Jewish Experience on the College Campus" held at Hebrew Union College-Jewish Institute of Religion on March 25, 1982. There, Professor Moshe Davis, Academic Chairman of the International Center for University Teaching of Jewish Civilization and Founding Head of the Institute of Contemporary Jewry, described two central problems faced by instructors who teach "The American Jewish Experience" on college campuses across the nation:

(1) Many who teach the subject specialize in other areas, some of them far removed from it, and complain of being inadequately prepared.

(2) Pedagogical materials dealing with American Jewry's past and present, and suitable for use in a college classroom, scarcely exist.

The American Jewish Experience Curriculum Project, jointly sponsored by the International Center for University Teaching of Jewish Civilization, Jerusalem, Israel and the Center for the Study of the American Jewish Experience on the campus of Hebrew Union College-Jewish Institute of Religion, Cincinnati, Ohio, was established to tackle both of these problems. *Jews and the Founding of the Republic*, a volume of collected and edited sources is its first offering. While not in itself a curriculum, as a resource package it contains materials usable in any number of ways and appropriate for students on various levels, instructors of various backgrounds, and for courses of various shapes and sizes. We hope that the resources it makes available will prove valuable to the public generally, and especially to teachers.

Dr. Jonathan D. Sarna, Associate Professor of American Jewish History at Hebrew Union College-Jewish Institute of Religion and Academic Director of its Center for the Study of the American Jewish Experience, directs the American Jewish Experience Curriculum Project. He co-edited the writing of this volume with Dr. Benny Kraut, Associate Professor and Director of the Judaic Studies Program at the University of Cincinnati. Dr. Sarna assumed primary responsibility for units 1, 2, 4 and 5; Dr. Kraut for units 3 and 6. Dr. Samuel Joseph, Associate Professor of Jewish Education and the project's Consultant in Education, produced the Guide to Resources and Materials, the index, and reviewed the units as they appeared. Special thanks for assistance and advice go to Dr. Jacob R. Marcus, Director of the American Jewish Archives, and to Dr. Abraham J. Peck, Associate Director. President Alfred Gottschalk of Hebrew Union College-Jewish Institute of Religion and Professor Moshe Davis initiated this project, participated in its organization, and have enthusiastically supported it throughout. Whatever success the project achieves stands in large part as a tribute to their vision.

An experimental edition of this volume was produced in 1983. It was then subjected to searching criticism by Professors Roger Daniels (University of Cincinnati), Todd Endelman (Indiana University), Lynn D. Gordon (University of Rochester), and Harold Wechsler (University of Chicago). While not all of their valuable suggestions could be incorporated into this revision, all proved helpful. Naturally, the editors alone assume final responsibility for any errors.

Last, but by no means least, we express our gratitude to the Joseph and Ceil Mazer Endowment Fund, created by the Jewish Communal Fund from a bequest of the Mazer Estate. The endowment's generous grant has made possible much of the early work of the Center for the Study of the American Jewish Experience. This volume, the "first fruits" of our efforts, is a memorial to the Mazer family's many years of support for Jewish causes. We are also greatly indebted to the Memorial Foundation for Jewish Culture for helping to underwrite the cost of this volume's publication in final form.

A NOTE TO TEACHERS

This volume proceeds from a basic belief that the American Jewish experience deserves a place in the school curriculum both as a separate course and integrated into existing courses devoted to American, Jewish and world history. Since curricular materials in American Jewish history scarcely exist, and since many libraries possess only the most rudimentary Judaica Americana collections, curriculum resource packages designed for instructors need to be created. *Jews and the Founding of the Republic* represents our initial effort to do just that as part of a larger curriculum project.

As a curriculum resource package, this volume includes material suitable both for a wide variety of instructors, specialists to non-specialists, and for a wide variety of courses, focused seminars to broad surveys. It provides primary sources, secondary sources, maps, illustrations, bibliographies, and a guide to available resources and materials. It is designed to be used in ways as diverse as are the needs of the different instructors which it seeks to serve.

We have divided *Jews and the Founding of the Republic* into six sections, beginning with a short background unit containing an article on colonial American Jewry and a survey overview of some of the topics elaborated upon later in the volume. The next four sections deal, respectively, with Jews and the coming of the Revolution, Jews in the Revolution, the impact of the Revolution on American Jews, and the relationship between the new nation and the Jewish community. Section Six, "Biblical Imagery and the Revolution," covers a related theme with which students need to be familiar.

Depending on the time available to them, instructors planning lectures on these subjects can work from either the primary or secondary sources provided. Documents can be photocopied for classroom analysis, and students can be directed for additional sources to items listed in the bibliography. Illustrations and audio-visual sources, listed in the guide, can be used for class enrichment.

In addition to setting forth the basic facts of American Jewish history, several major themes emerge from this volume which may be highlighted in a classroom presentation. We pose them here as a series of five questions:

(1) How was the American Jewish experience in the Revolution like and unlike that of Americans generally?

(2) How did the founding of the Republic affect the subsequent course of Jewish history in America?

(3) In what ways does the history of the founding of the Republic demonstrate American exceptionalism with regard to Jews? In what ways was America just like European countries?

(4) How did being Jewish affect one's being an American in the early Republic? How did being an American affect one's being Jewish?

(5) How was the American Jewish experience in the Revolution similar to and different from the American Jewish experience today?

Of course, this list lays no claim to being exhaustive. Instructors will discover in *Jews and the Founding of the Republic* data bearing on other questions as well. What we have tried to stress, however, is the importance of viewing the American Jewish experience in its broadest context: as the interrelationship between the narrow history of American Jews and the wider currents of American, Jewish and world historical developments. Lending significance to the topic in this way avoids many of the dangers traditionally associated with "minority group history." It permits American Jewish history to be viewed as it should be viewed: as part of the larger mosaic that is our collective past.

INTRODUCTION

An earlier generation of American Jewish historians studied the Revolutionary era in order to find Jewish heroes. They worked assiduously to locate the name of every Jew who fought for the patriotic cause, and stressed the contributions to American freedom made by such men as Haym Salomon, whose activities as a broker brought much-needed funds into the new nation's treasury. Today, American Jewish historians have other concerns. What is most important to them, as this volume demonstrates, is the *total* experience of Jews in the Revolution, how that experience was like and unlike that of other Americans, how it differed from the experience of Jews elsewhere, and how it affected the whole future course of American Jewish life.

As we now know, the American Revolution marked a turning point not only in American Jewish history, but in modern Jewish history generally. Never before had a major nation committed itself so definitively to the principles of democracy and freedom in general, and to religious freedom in particular. The Constitution's twin assurances -- that "no religious test shall ever be required as a qualification to an office or public trust under the United States (Article VI)," and that "Congress shall make no law respecting an establishment of religion, or prohibiting the free exercise thereof (Amendment 1)" -- meant for Jews that they could claim true equality in America, not mere toleration as was accorded them in even the most liberal of European countries. Religious pluralism had become a reality in America. Jews and members of other minority religions could dissent from the religious views of the majority without fear of persecution.

Momentous as this guarantee of legal equality was, it did not immediately translate for Jews into full social equality. As several documents in this volume demonstrate, Jews still had to fight for their rights on the state level, and they continued to face various forms of prejudice nationwide. Yet at the same time, as other documents here demonstrate, many Jews benefited materially from the Revolution and interacted freely with their non-Jewish neighbors. This much at least can be said with certainty: Having shed blood for their country side by side with their fellow Christians, Jews as a group felt far more secure than they had in colonial days. They asserted their rights openly, and if challenged, defended themselves both vigorously and self-confidently.

The changes wrought by the Constitution, the effort to weave Jews into the fabric of the nation's social and religious life, and the early struggles to maintain a Jewish lifestyle in the midst of a non-Jewish environment all serve as background to themes that appear over and over in the annals of American Jewish history. The number of Jews residing in America during this period may have been small, but the problems they faced were similar to those that Jews would always face in America's free environment. For this reason, the impact that the American Revolution had on American Jews is critical. It set in motion many of the forces that helped to shape the American Jewish community forever after.

A PROFILE OF AMERICAN JEWS AT THE TIME OF THE AMERICAN REVOLUTION

Population: 1500-2500 (.05% - .10% of America's total population of between 2.5 million and 3 million)

Main Countries of Origin:
   Spain, Portugal, Holland, Italy (= *Sephardim*)
   Poland, Hungary, Germany, Lithuania (= *Ashkenazim*)
   Note: Many Jewish immigrants came to the United States *after* living in England or the Caribbean colonies. By the Revolution, *there were more Ashkenazim in America than Sephardim*. The Sephardic prayer ritual nevertheless continued to predominate.

Major Settlements:

   Newport

   New York

   Philadelphia

   Charleston

   Savannah

   Montreal

Synagogue Buildings:

   Shearith Israel (New York - **1730**)

   Yeshuat Israel (Newport - **1763**)

   Shearith Israel (Montreal - **1777**)

   Mikveh Israel (Philadelphia - **1782**)

   Beth Elohim (Charleston - **1780** (rented quarters), **1794** (own building))

Major Occupations:

   merchants

   traders

Number of Jews Who Fought in Revolution: about **100** (various ranks)

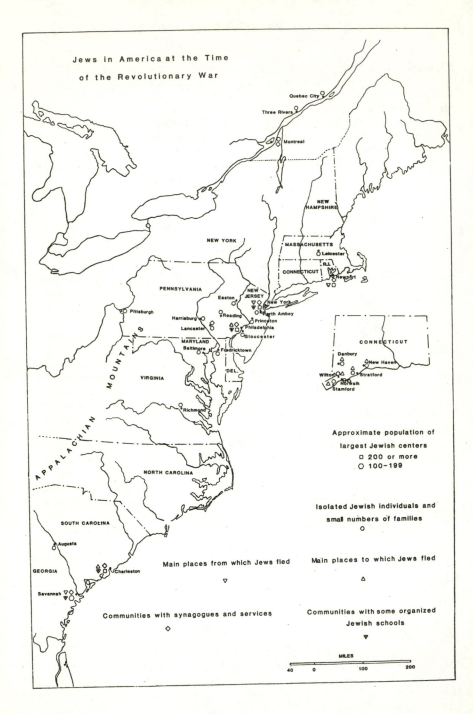

Jews in America at the Time
of the Revolutionary War

Quebec City
Three Rivers
Montreal

NEW HAMPSHIRE

NEW YORK

MASSACHUSETTS
Leicester
R.I.
CONNECTICUT
Newport

PENNSYLVANIA
Easton
NEW JERSEY
New York
Pittsburgh   Reading   Perth Amboy
Harrisburg   Princeton
Lancaster   Philadelphia
MARYLAND   Gloucester
Baltimore   Fredricktown

CONNECTICUT
Danbury
Wilton   New Haven
Stratford
Norwalk
Stamford

DEL.
VIRGINIA

Richmond

NORTH CAROLINA

SOUTH CAROLINA

Augusta

GEORGIA
Charleston
Savannah

Approximate population of
largest Jewish centers
☐ 200 or more
○ 100–199

Isolated Jewish individuals and
small numbers of families
○

Main places from which Jews fled
▽

Main places to which Jews fled
△

Communities with synagogues and services
◇

Communities with some organized
Jewish schools
▼

MILES
40   0   100   200

CHAPTER I

BACKGROUND

Jews had lived in America for more than a century before the American Revolution. A group of twenty-three Jewish refugees from Recife, Brazil landed in New Amsterdam, later known as New York, in 1654. Later, through the decades, particularly in the eighteenth century, enterprising Jews of Sephardic (Spanish-Jewish tradition) and then increasingly Ashkenazic (German-Polish-Jewish tradition) background migrated to the American colonies in search of opportunity and refuge. Unlike most other immigrants of the period, Jews established themselves in the developing urban seacoast cities from Savannah to Newport. For the most part they earned their living through commerce and trade. Although numerically they remained an infinitesimal part of the population (between one in every one thousand and one in every two thousand Americans was Jewish), individual Jews did play highly important roles in community affairs. In Newport, for example, Aaron Lopez stood in the 1770s as "a merchant of the first eminence," one of the wealthiest and most powerful men in all Rhode Island. Jews still labored under legal disabilities in the colonies, and as members of a minority faith they encountered prejudice and discrimination. But overall, by 1776 Jews had rooted themselves in America and found in various colonies both the security and the success that they had been seeking.

THE COLONIAL AMERICAN JEW

Jacob R. Marcus

Jacob R. Marcus presents here a synoptic overview of colonial American Jewry, particularly as Jews related to the overall American community of the period. Marcus has written the basic work entitled The Colonial American Jew *(3 volumes, Detroit, 1970) in which he deals at length with colonial Jewry's settlement patterns, legal and political status, economic activities, religious life, and relations with other Americans. This article summarizes his most important findings and sets the stage for developments to come.*

Mid-twentieth century American Jewry is the largest Jewish community in the world. Ancient Israel in her palmiest days sheltered but a fraction of the millions that are now to be found in America's largest cities. Where did these people come from?

The first American Jews originated in Europe. By the sixteenth century, most Jews in Western Europe had been forcibly deprived of their ancestral faith and identity; an indeterminate number had been driven underground as crypto-Jews. In Central Europe many had been killed or expelled from their homes, and some had migrated eastward, beyond the Oder River, into the towns, villages, and hamlets of sprawling Poland. The Thirty Years' War, which wracked the Germanies during the 1600s, brought the East Europeans additional emigres, but in 1648, when that tragic struggle came to an end, new conflicts - beginning with the revolt of the Cossacks - broke out in the Slavic lands. For the first time in centuries, then, the tide of immigration began to move not eastward, but westward.

There was no choice for the Jews; they had to turn west, for Russia was closed to them, and Western Europe had begun to take on a new lease of life. Modernism was dawning there politically, economically, and culturally, and the states between the Pyrenees and the Oder River, seeking to rebuild themselves along national mercantilist lines, were now more sympathetic to immigrants with skills. Men and wealth were needed to speed the Commercial Revolution and to people the new colonies in the Atlantic basin. Venturesome Jews from East European lands moved into Germany, Holland, and England, and Iberians of Jewish ancestry crossed the Pyrenees into France or sailed for Amsterdam, Hamburg, and London. Most Jews who wandered into this new and rehabilitated Western Europe were happy to remain. They could anticipate a promising future. A few, however, spilled over into the American colonies.

Actually, "Jews" - people of Jewish origin - had been settling in the Western Hemisphere since at least the early 1500s. The very first

Marranos came with Columbus, and in less than a century they had spread throughout the Caribbean and found their way into Mexico (New Spain) and South America, but the Inquisition made it impossible for them to establish viable communities. It was not until the mid-1600s that the first overt Jewish settlements sprang up in the New World - in Dutch Brazil and Surinam, on Curacao, and on English Barbados and Jamaica. These were soon to become large and cultured metropolitan communities, for the Caribbean basin was at the time far more attractive and more populous than the mainland provinces to the north. The most important American Jewries of the eighteenth century were to develop in Surinam and in the Islands.

When the Portuguese recaptured Brazil, a handful of Dutch Jews, fleeing north, found refuge in the Dutch trading colony of New Amsterdam, soon to become English New York. Their arrival on the Hudson in 1654 represents the beginning of North American Jewish life. These twenty-three Jewish "Pilgrim Fathers" were followed during the next hundred years by immigrants from the Islands and from Spain, Portugal, France, Holland, Germany, and England. By 1730, Jews of Central European origin outnumbered their Iberian coreligionists in North America. The first settlers in the 1600s were characteristically traders who had little desire to remain, but a permanent community had been established by the turn of the century. The Jewish businessmen married, settled down, and began to raise families. Throughout the colonial period, however, American Jewry would remain an essentially immigrant group. Up to the Revolution, some 70 percent of the presidents of the New York synagogue were foreign-born, and the men who assumed leadership of colonial American Jewish life were, with one notable exception, all immigrants. Many of the emigres were competent merchandisers. Some of them had distinguished rabbinical ancestors; a few were unassorted misfits. The community's growth is reflected in the fact that there were about 250 Jews on the continent by the year 1700, whereas, by 1776, there were about 2,500. Jews never formed more than one-tenth of 1 percent of the colonial population.

What prompted Jewish newcomers to set sail across the Atlantic? Was it a quest for religious freedom? The fact is that even the Dutch exiles from Brazil and the Spanish-Portuguese emigres of converso ancestry who fled the Iberian Peninsula were not drawn to North American shores primarily for the sake of conscience; all of them could have found a haven in other lands, and if they came here, it was more often than not to better themselves economically. Nearly all of them sought, in addition, a measure of anonymity, an avoidance of public notice, for without exception they came from lands which still imposed disabilities on Jews and still enforced anti-Jewish laws of a medieval character. It is understood, of course, that these men would not have come to these shores if they had not been allowed to practice their faith. The immigrants took it for granted that they would be permitted to establish a community of their own.

Where did they settle? Some, to be sure, were found in the hinterland, but even they had trickled into the backcountry through the seacoast towns. Most Jews stayed well below the piedmont, in the tidewater areas. New Amsterdam-New York was the first and chief Jewish center, but only a short generation after the Brazilians arrived, a small settlement took shape at Newport, in the 1680s at the latest. That Rhode Island community did not last even a decade, however, and it was not until the 1740s that the New Yorkers, fanning out once again, reestablished Jewish life in Newport. Jewish newcomers, moving north, rarely bypassed the Rhode Island city; they tended to ignore Boston; apparently one center in New England sufficed them. That same decade of the 1740s saw the New Yorkers, in their southward trek, lay the foundations for a community at Philadelphia. Independently of New York, Charleston Jewry also established itself in the 1740s. Savannah, which had sheltered a substantial number of Jewish colonists in the 1730s, had already lost her first Jewish group by 1740, but, like Newport, would ultimately rebuild a durable Jewish settlement on the dead hopes of earlier emigres. After the French and Indian War, New Yorkers moved up the Hudson and Lake Champlain to found a new congregation in Montreal.

It is obvious that nowhere in the fourteen provinces were Jews qua Jews ever openly denied the right to strike roots. By 1740, they were allowed the exercise of virtually every economic immunity and privilege. Not that such rights were obtained without a struggle! The Dutch in New Amsterdam, under the medieval-minded Stuyvesant, sought to deny them nearly all rights; yet it took no more than three years for them to wrest from the governor and his superiors in the Dutch West India Company the right to remain, to trade, to own land, and to hold worship services in private. These rights were extended under English rule, so that, even before the coming of the new century, England had, however reluctantly, accorded her American Jewish subjects full civil equality. In 1740, an imperial naturalization law confirmed the status of the Jew and offered him almost unlimited economic opportunity in the Empire as a whole as well as in the American provinces themselves.

Civil equality was not, of course, political equality. Jews in some colonies were certainly allowed the vote on a provincial and a local level, but they were nowhere permitted to hold honorific office. Such office was limited to Protestant Christians, especially those associated with the dominant or established church in each colony. On the whole, prior to the 1760s, the American Jew eschewed politics. Fourteen hundred years of Christian-imposed disabilities had taught him that political plums like lucrative offices were not within his reach, but his disability does not appear to have disturbed him before 1765. After all, the constant wars, the country's expanding economy, and the penetration of the West enabled the Jewish businessman to make a good living; he was simply too busy building an estate for himself and his family to concern himself with the fact that political appointments were denied him.

Still, when he was offered important communal committee assign-
ments, he would seem to have gladly accepted them. Almost every
town had some Jewish merchants of substance and wealth, and in the
English world of mercantilism, the Jewish businessman, even if he
could not sit in the Assembly, on the bench, or in the provincial council, was undeniably a part of the power structure. In Continental
Europe, he could not have aspired to authority in the general community, for Jewry as an ethnic corporation was segregated by tradition and
by the terms of separatist and divisive *privilegia*. The colonial Jew,
however, followed the developing pattern of English Jewry; he aspired
to enter the general society within the ambit of a common unitary political system. He was not averse to office, to its opportunities, and its
responsibilities, nor was he indifferent to the improvement of his
status. Ultimately the Jew here hoped to become one, politically at
least, with the emerging American people and to be accepted as a full
fellow-citizen, but he was willing to bide his time. And his hopes
achieved fulfillment, if as yet mainly on the federal level, in 1789.

The Jew of eighteenth-century America found his greatest opportunity in the world of commerce. Here, much more so than on the Continent, or even in England, he was almost exclusively a shopkeeper. To
be sure, there were occasional dirt farmers in the northern provinces,
and even an aristocratic planter on the South Carolina frontier, but
farming was not the metier of these immigrants. Georgia Jewish merchants might hold good-sized ranches in the backcountry, and craftsmen, especially silversmiths, might be found in nearly every province,
but the typical Jew was a businessman who owned a small shop. There
he doled out credit to the customers who came to him for hardware,
hard liquor, and dry goods. The successful shopkeeper became a merchant, and large-scale Jewish storekeepers were established even in the
villages of Canada and as far west as Lancaster, Pennsylvania. The
Montreal businessmen were primarily fur entrepeneurs, and
Lancaster's outstanding merchant was well known as a supplier for the
traders on the Ohio.

The important Jews in commerce were the tidewater merchant-
shippers of Newport, New York, and Philadelphia. They exchanged
American foods and forest products in Europe and the West Indies for
consumer goods and for Caribbean staples like molasses, rum, sugar,
and dyewoods. Sometimes, like the Jew who was Newport's commercial
tycoon, they would participate in the African slave trade. Jewish
merchant-shippers of that day were also industrialists, arranging
through the put-out system for the manufacture of ships and barrels,
the distillation of rum, the catching and processing of fish and whales,
and the production of kosher and unkosher victuals for export. Above
all, they were in the candle business. Indeed, it is no exaggeration to
say that they constituted an important national factor in the manufacture of candles. Jews, however, were notably absent from the iron and

tobacco industries, and though they included in their ranks substantial merchant-shippers, the total volume of their business, while it far exceeded their proportion to the population, was hardly determining in any field. The one exception, it might be said, was army supply: The most powerful Jewish commercial clan of the third quarter of the century was an Anglo-American family of army purveyors which reached its zenith during the French and Indian War. Like its Jewish counterparts in Europe, this clan carried on business operations reaching, at the very least, into the hundreds of thousands, if not millions, of pounds.

It may be fairly maintained that all but an infinitesimal number of North American Jews were to be included in a broadly-conceived middle class. Some Jewish merchants were even wealthy by contemporary standards; practically none of the Jews were paupers, very few were proletarians, and a substantial number were lower-middle-class petit bourgeois shopkeepers and middle-middle-class storekeepers and merchants. There were very few Jews who did not enjoy a degree of comfort; most of them made a "good living" and survived economically, though severe business reverses were by no means uncommon among them at some time or other.

The colonial American Jewish community could be accurately described as a socioreligious group - or even a religiosocial group - whose members had grown up, for the most part, in the small towns of pre-industrial Europe. Though they stopped to make no sharp distinctions between the religious and the secular, their orientation was definitely religious, and they were typically synagoguegoers. On their arrival here, they had immediately undertaken to set up de facto communities whose hub was, in every case, the house of worship. It was in a literal sense a meetinghouse. All newcomers were expected to join, to become paying members, or at least to attend the important services. Local Jewry was granted no state authority to compel membership, but social pressure generally saw to it that affiliation would be practically compulsory.

Even though religious devotions were undoubtedly held in every Jewish settlement as soon as the requisite quorum of ten adult males thirteen years of age or older could be mustered, the synagogue was not actually the first institution to be established. The first formal act was usually the acquisition of a plot of ground for a cemetery. Then came the synagogue. First the worshippers would rent a room, then a house; then they would purchase a building, and, finally, they would erect a synagogue of their own. The synagogue-communal organization was of the simplest type, featuring a president, a small board, and at times a treasurer. Frequently, the overburdened chief executive served also as secretary and treasurer; the major administrative duties were his. No rabbis - that is, no ordained, learned, professional officiants - were employed in North America prior to the second quarter of the nineteenth century. Colonial Jewry had no need for the services of experts to teach rabbinic lore to advanced students, or to sit as judges to adjudicate complex commercial disputes and matters touching on marriage, divorce, and estates. The chief salaried - or volunteer - officiant in every house of worship was the cantor who chanted the liturgy. His ministrations were complemented by those of the *shohet*, who slaughtered food animals ritually, and the beadle, who served as the omnibus factotum for the board. These functionaries were certainly not overpaid, and all of them engaged in some form of gainful enterprise, on the side, to augment their incomes.

The liturgy employed by all the colonial conventicles was the Sephardic or Spanish-Portuguese. Despite the fact that prerevolutionary American Jewry was overwhelmingly Ashkenazic (German-Polish) in ethnic origin, the Sephardic style had become the traditional American rite. Services were almost always held on the Sabbath and on all the holidays, though the difficulty of assembling ten busy adults often made it impossible to organize daily services. Ceremonial and ritual observance was expected of all Jews, even of those who lived in the backcountry, and the communal leaders attempted to exact conformity by threatening ecclesiastical punishments. The board was - or at least attempted to be - an authoritative body exercising discipline in religious matters over every confessing Jew in the region, but, unlike some of the Protestant sects, there was no effort to exercise surveillance in business concerns or even in the area of personal morals.

In the extant budgets of the country's chief synagogue, the largest items were salaries, pensions, and relief for the poor. It is true that congregants squabbled among themselves, often bitterly and vindictively, but generous provision was nearly always made for the needy and the impoverished. The Jews took care of their own. Itinerants from the distant Islands were "dispatched" back home at communal expense; Palestinian visitors were generously entertained and given gifts; and aspiring petitioners were granted modest loans to set them up in business. The sick received medical care, nursing, and hospitalization; the old were pensioned, and all the dead were buried at the expense of the community or for a purely nominal fee. Most Protestant groups also attempted to take care of their poor. Whether the Jews did more for their people than, for instance, Protestant sectarians like the Quakers, is difficult to determine, though a comparative study of budgets might answer this question.

Only to a limited degree was education associated with charity. Since the local community always included members who lacked the means to educate their children, the synagogal authorities never failed to provide a subsidized teacher for the children of the poor. Actually, however, the responsibility for providing instruction was the obligation of the head of the household; it was not a communal responsibility. Beyond question there had been private Hebrew instructors in New York City ever since the seventeenth century, and a communal Hebrew school was organized during the 1730s, at the latest, with all who had means paying tuition. Not all the children in the community had resort to the congregational school. Even in New York City - and this was certainly true of all the other Jewish communities as well - secular education was also acquired in private schools or through tutors.

The curriculum of the congregational school probably included the reading and translation of the prayer book and the Pentateuch, and at most some familiarity with the classical biblical commentaries. By the 1750s, this Hebrew school had become an all-day "publick school" teaching Spanish and the three "Rs" - what we might call a "parochial" school. The language of instruction was English. The quality of the teaching in Hebrew was probably not too bad, for the first American-trained cantor is known to have had the capacity to consult the more elementary Hebrew codes. We have no way to gauge the quality of the instruction in "English reading, writing, and cyphering," but, since all Jewish children, even the humblest among them, were prepared for some form of business life, it may be assumed that the training the young natives acquired was adequate. Male immigrants with very few exceptions were literate. They could read English, write it phonetically at least, and keep a set of books. All were bilingual, for they knew English and Yiddish or German, or English and Spanish or Portuguese. A few had a third language at their command - Dutch, for instance - and some, if not many, were multilingual.

Exceedingly few young people were tempted to attend the country's colleges, although secondary schools were open to them in Rhode Island, New York, and Pennsylvania. Most colonial Jews were not interested in the liberal arts as such, and professional training in law and medicine was not sought. The practice of medicine was not particularly lucrative, while lawyers were in bad repute throughout much of this period, and, if English precedent was determining, Jews would not have been permitted to practice in the courts. Prior to 1776, the American Jew wrote nothing in English worth preserving as a literary monument. The typical colonial synagoguegoer, an immigrant, was too busy learning the language and making a living to achieve any facility or distinction in English letters; he could make no contribution even to the Jewish, let alone American, literary arts.

What did their neighbors think of the Jews? Every Christian who came to these shores brought with him "invisible baggage": his European and pagan traditions going back for millennia. The West India Company in New Amsterdam never hid its distaste for Jews; the New York rabble, headed by a "gentleman," attacked a Jewish funeral cortege on one occasion, and the desecration of cemeteries was not uncommon. "Jew" was still a dirty word, and it was hardly rare to see the Jews denigrated as such in the press. A distinguished lawyer speaking in the New York General Assembly did not find it too difficult to rouse his fellow-members against the Jews as a people guilty of the great crime of the Crucifixion.

Rejection does not tell the whole story, however, and one always does well to bear it in mind that, if the Jewish businessman prospered in this land, it was because the Gentiles patronized him. Jews did not make a living by taking in each other's washing. There can be no question that the Jews here found more acceptance than in any other land in the world. Old-World traditions of Judeophobia were attenuated here. The Christian drama of salvation - a drama in which the Jew played the villain - was not dominant in moulding public opinion in the colonies, for America offered everyone opportunity enough; there was no need to envy the Jew. In a society of Dunkers, Congregationalists, Moravian Brethren, Baptists, Christian Sabbatarians, Catholics, Methodists, Anglicans, Presbyterians (Old Side and New Side), Lutherans, Dutch Reformed, German Reformed, Mennonites, Schwenkfelders, a society of English, Scottish, Irish, German, Dutch, Welsh, Swiss and Swedish settlers - not to mention Negroes and Indians - the Jew did not stand out too conspicuously. Christians in the villages and towns of the country discovered, sometimes to their dismay, that the Jews did not wear horns and that, if they had devil's tails and cloven feet, these were certainly not visible. The Christian who learned to know Mr. Judah, or Mr. Josephson, or Mr. Hays, or Mr. Gratz found that, after all, he was not so different, and the Jew was accepted. If he became a son-in-law, he was welcomed; he was a fine fellow.

The Jew was accepted, but did he accept America? What was this man like? What was happening to him on this side of the Atlantic? Was he different here? What had he gained for himself? What did he do for others, for this country which generously gave him a haven and a new home?

Apparently he was still the same "eternal" Jew, still the European traditionalist, equally untouched by deism and by Protestant religiosity, whether of the decorous Anglican kind or of the less conventional emotionalism of the Great Awakening. Yet he *was* different, if only because he found himself in a different milieu, and this was bound to influence and change him. It was not simply that, instead of speaking Yiddish or a bad German, he now spoke fractured English and dressed like any middle-class Englishman. This young American Jewish community of which he was a loyal and exuberant member shaped itself on a "frontier" far removed from the European *Judengasse* and its age-old classical traditions. The New World challenged his Old World. In order to survive here, the Jew found it expedient to extemporize, to compromise, and all this, in the final analysis, spelt a form of emancipation. Europe had never offered him more than a second-class citizenship; here in America, however, he encountered less paternalism and a more sympathetic government. Here, after 1700, he had full civil liberties and even a degree of civic recognition. By 1775, he had come very close to achieving first-class citizenship.

America connoted economic opportunity, and this was of paramount importance: "Bread to eat and a garment to wear." He was no longer a peddler, a petty trader, a cattle dealer; he was now a shop-keeper, even a merchant. If only because of the "wealth" he was often enough enabled to accumulate in America, he became something of a community figure. Here he could rise on the social ladder; he could improve his status and even enter into the world of Anglo-Saxon education and culture. Here the Jewish heritage reached out to absorb a new language and new ideals: "democracy," "natural freedom," "dictates of humanity," "constitutional trial by jury," "to live free or not at all," "rights, liberties and immunities." He had acquired a new vocabulary.

When the Jew left Europe, he left behind him there - physically at least - the all-pervasive authority of the Jewish community. Ultimately, his departure from the European home was to effect a measure of spiritual distance as well. If Jewish orthodoxy in its most classical form was to be found then in Poland, the Jews of these colonies were as remote from it physically as a sailing vessel could carry them. America signified the ultimate frontier of Jewish life. Religious controls were inevitably relaxed here. There was much less concern about observance and ritual. The individual was far freer to do as he pleased. He could if he wished - and most commonly he did wish - pay much less attention to the rabbinic learning which, for a thousand years, had been the leit-motif of European Jewish life. The new American Jew, who was beginning to emerge on the colonial scene, much preferred to be a successful merchant than a talmudic scholar. Yet this very Jew was not estranged from his faith, and the communities which studded the North American coast from Montreal to Savannah are eloquent testimony to his determination not to abandon his heritage.

The typical colonial Jew was true to his heritage because he was not pressed to be untrue to it. There was no overwhelming, mono-chromatic culture here to force itself upon him. There was no national ethos to exact conformity of him. If he acculturated, it was by his own choice. Free here to express his religious loyalties, since the outside world imposed no religious limitations upon him and extorted no price of emancipation, he assimilated almost unwittingly and without hesitation. Slowly but surely he sloughed off Europe. He felt completely at home here. The Jewish immigrant - and this was very probably not characteristic of him alone - manifested an aptitude for acculturation and even for total integration. Bear in mind that he had come originally from a Portuguese city, a German *Dorf*, or a Polish hamlet; yet, when he appeared as an urban businessman, he was already an urbane American. He had speedily become acquainted with English amenities and often had even acquired an Anglo-Saxon name. If he finally settled in a colonial village, it was usually only a matter of time before he married a Christian and permitted his wife to rear his children as she thought fit. But conversion to Judaism, formal or informal on the part of the woman, might also occur, though with much less frequency. In a way, it is astounding how easy it was for many an observant European Jew to foreswear in a few years nearly twenty-seven centuries of hallowed tradition - seemingly without a struggle.

The Jew *was* different here. He had left the "ghetto" to become a pioneer on the American "frontier," a frontier which according to Frederick Jackson Turner gave its people

> coarseness and strength combined with acuteness and inquisitiveness; that practical, inventive turn of mind, quick to find expedients; that masterful grasp of material things, lacking in the artistic but powerful to effect great ends; that restless, nervous energy; that dominant individualism, working for good and for evil, and withal that buoyancy and exuberance which comes with freedom.

For Turner, the frontier which effected these changes in the American psyche was the "Great West." Yet a moment's reflection will remind the student that these enumerated characteristics bespeak the successful American businessman, Jew or Christian. Think of Thomas Hancock! Certainly for the professing Jew - who was never to become a backwoods hunter or an Indian fighter - all of America was a frontier. If to be a frontiersman is to be a man who dares to hazard, then the Jews as a whole are America's urban frontiersmen par excellence. As a group, they are, more than others, a "nation of shopkeepers," gambling with their future. (Actually, of course, the Diaspora Jew had always lived as a marginal man on the "cutting edge," where he had to struggle for survival juridically, commercially, and spiritually.) The Western frontier is in no sense important for the development of the American Jew; the Atlantic frontier is all important. It was determinative in changing him. It gave him his greatest opportunity in centures to give free play to those traits which he had already brought with him and which had long been characteristic of him.

For the Jew, the style of life was different here. He learned to dispense with Slavic obsequiousness and Germanic servility. There was no need for him here to be submissive. Here he could be assertive - if that was his nature. If he possessed physical courage, America offered him ample opportunity to manifest it. He learned not to be easily cowed. Is there any doubt that it required moral courage to cross the broad ocean and to traverse the lofty mountains and the dark forests to distant Michilimackinac or the Forks of the Ohio? For the first time in centuries, the Jew felt free. He was no longer faced with the problem of treading softly in the presence of a virulent Judeophobia. It may have been hard for him, but he began to trust his Christian neighbors; he became less suspicious of them. They were his customers; often enough they were his partners in business ventures, and he learned to believe in them, for there is no intimacy greater than that of two men who are prepared to share profits and losses.

The Jew of the European village who could only dream of a great future had the chance here to prove his mettle. He could be venturesome, daring, and enterprising. Here there was an open road for the man of ambition. It was not ludicrous here to project gargantuan schemes. No one looked askance at the Christian-Jewish consortium which proposed to establish a western colony of millions upon millions of acres. America was one land where, more than any other, the Jew could fulfill his inmost self by attempting whatever career he wished. Here he could be an individual. With opportunity and achievement and the regard of others came self-respect and dignity. The Jewish merchant was conscious of his own works; he knew what he was doing for the land and the people - and it was good in his eyes. He was giving and getting. He had the pride of a merchant, and he expected recognition, not only socially, but in rights and in privileges.

It is undeniable: The American Jewish businessman *was* more than a European who dressed and spoke like an Anglo-Saxon. His children, too, were different. The father may have been a Spaniard or a Pole or a native Briton, but the children through intramarriage with Jews of other backgrounds were something new. This was a Jewish melting pot which fused together the Jews of half of Europe's lands to produce a new ethnic type - an "American" Jew. This American Jew "in becoming" struck a balance between his European religiocultural loyalties and his emotional identification with the spirit of this land. In Europe, he had been an outsider; in this land, he blended with the others. Here there were a dozen different breeds and stocks pouring into one another to become one in a common environment with common interests. This man was among that dozen, and though he would never have admitted it, he was becoming less of a Jew and more of an American.

In 1711, a number of New York's Jewish businessmen generously contributed to the building of an Anglican church; some fifty years later, the Jews of Savannah were active in a nondenominational charitable society. Such participation by Jews in American philanthropy can take on meaning only if we remember that in most European lands at that time the Jew was still held in disdain and that in some countries he was even outlawed and in danger of massacre. But here in the colonies, he believed, he knew, that he was part of the body politic. It is true that he had his own way of life, but, unlike others, particularly some of the Germans, he never locked himself behind the walls of a cultural enclave. Of course, he was fully conscious of the fact that he was not yet a first-class citizen. He realized it only too well, but his resentment never impelled him to withdraw into himself. He was very much moved by the political unrest of his neighbors and shared their hopes. Like all dissenters and all who labored under legal disabilities, he was not satisfied with the status quo; he sought more rights and more opportunities. A large measure of freedom had already been accorded him, but the Revolutionary spirit of the 1760s unleashed in him the desire for an even larger measure. It was this hope that prompted Jews to throw in their lot with the Whigs. By 1775, even many of the most recent newcomers thought of themselves as Americans, and "as a man thinketh in his heart, so is he."

By 1776, the typical Jew in this land was an urban shopkeeper of German provenance in the process of blotting out his German ethnic past. Yet he was firmly, proudly, and nostalgically rooted in his European religious traditions. He spoke English by preference, had regard for Anglo-Saxon culture, and enjoyed the same civil rights as did his Christian neighbors. Socially, he was a cut above the masses, the farmers and the mechanics, for he was a shopkeeper or merchant. As such, he expected - and he received - a measure of deference.

What did this man achieve for himself? He moved Europe across the Atlantic, no mean achievement. Synagogues, schools, charities, a "community" were transferred here, nailed down and fastened, firm and viable and visible enough to attract hundreds and thousands of others who never would have come to a "waste howling wilderness" where there were no Jewish institutions. A dozen families in seventeenth-century New York laid the foundations for a twentieth-century community of nearly six million Jews. Colonial Jewry wrote the pattern of acculturation which made it possible for the Jew to remain a Jew and to become an American. The pioneers of the eighteenth century succeeded in making an exemplary transition from a still medieval European Jewish life to the new American world of modernism and personal freedom.

What did this man achieve for the land? Not that this Jew was conscious of it, but together with all dissenters - and every American denomination suffered disabilities in one or another of the provinces - he helped teach his neighbor religious tolerance. The fruit of this tolerance was respect for the personality of the individual. The prerevolutionary Jew made no contribution to the literature of the colonies; he cleared no forests and ploughed no furrow - yet he, too, built the land. He, as much as any other, made American life more comfortable through the necessities and luxuries which he provided. It is true that the trader needed his customers, but it is equally true that neither city craftsmen nor toiling rustics could exist without him. It is true, too, that in a literal numerical sense the Jew was one man in a thousand, but, in an economy where an overwhelming majority of all who labored made their living on the soil, it is difficult to overstress the importance of the shopkeeper and the merchant.

SOURCE: Jacob R. Marcus, *The American Colonial Jew: A Study in Acculturation.* (B.G. Rudolph Lectures in Judaic Studies, Department of Religion, Syracuse University, 1967). Reprinted by permission of Jacob R. Marcus.

THE ROLE OF THE JEWS IN THE AMERICAN REVOLUTION

IN HISTORICAL PERSPECTIVE

Richard B. Morris

Richard Morris, one of America's leading historians, takes up where Marcus left off, and surveys major features of the Jewish experience in the American Revolution. Morris believes that the Jewish situation sheds light on broader aspects of the history of minority groups in America. He contrasts America's "toleration toward Jews and other religious minorities, and the steps taken to guarantee their civil and political rights," with "the nonaction on this subject in England" during the same period.

The story of the American Revolution is not complete without some acknowledgment of the role the Jews played in that conflict, and, in a broader sense, of the contribution of Jews and other minorities to the recognition of rights and values which are now considered an integral part of the American tradition.

Some fifty years ago an American President of New England origin, taking a phrase he attributed inaccurately to Lecky, paid tribute to the "Hebraic mortar which cemented the foundations of American democracy." Calvin Coolidge was acknowledging that strong sense of literary identification with the ancient people of Israel shared by Puritans and Pilgrims alike. The American Puritan tradition was immersed in Hebraism. A crucial and distinctive principle of its system - the covenant theology - is rooted in the Old Testament. The covenant theology was the keystone to the democratic control of church government under the Puritan Congregational system, and explains what looks like a revolutionary principle of government embodied in the Mayflower Compact, and in the settlements in Connecticut, New Hampshire, and Rhode Island. It is government based upon the consent of the people. This relationship between the Hebrew concept of the covenant and the Puritan concept is summed up in a remark of the Puritan thinker Joshua Moody: "We are all the children of Abraham; and therefore we are under Abraham's covenant."

Not only the Puritans but a later generation of Revolutionary Founding Fathers took almost daily inspiration from the Old Testament. John Jay, in his famous Address to the Convention of the State of New York in late 1776, argued that the persecution suffered by the American colonists at the hands of the British was worse than that suffered by the Jews from the tyrants of Egypt. Washington urged that the "most atrocious" war profiteers "be hung on gallows five times as high as Haman's," and innumerable like quotations from the Revolutionary years can be readily culled.

What these worthies are speaking about are the people of the book, not the Jews of flesh and blood of their own times, for many Americans, by the time of the Revolution, had probably never met a Jew. For the first hundred years or so of their existence in the colonies, the Jews constituted a minuscule minority. By the time of the Revolution there could not have been more than 2,000 Jews out of a total population of 2,500,000. At the start, then, the question might well be asked whether so tiny a minority could exercise a meaningful role in the great events that were about to transpire. In answering that question one should bear in mind that, though small in numbers, the Jews in America were literate, propertied, and often well connected, that they lived chiefly in the principal towns that were tinderboxes of revolt, and that the network of imperial blood relationships of which they formed a part gave them a special advantage in overseas transactions. One could say that they had a stake in the establishment without being a part thereof.

First of all, though, we should not allow filiopietism to blind us to a realization that the American Revolution, as a civil war, found Jews divided among themselves over support or resistance to revolt. Like other inhabitants of the colonies, Jews obeyed the dictates of conscience and exercised the right of dissent from whichever party might be the prevailing one in their particular communities. The coming of the Revolution found Jewish families, like those of other faiths, torn asunder and Jewish congregations split wide open. Perhaps most conspicuous on the Loyalist side was the Franks family of Philadelphia, one that lacked a strong sense of Jewish identity. Historians still narrate the role of Rebecca Franks, a society belle in her time, who acted as one of the two "Queens of Beauty" and graced an Italian medley which was performed in the Quaker City in the late spring of 1778 in honor of a departing and less-than-triumphant British general, Sir William Howe. Her father, David Franks, an outstanding merchant, played an ambivalent role during the Revolutionary crisis, his actions seemingly motivated by opportunism rather than conviction.

Appointed by the Continental Congress to serve as agent to supply American prisoners in British hands with provisions and other necessaries, he was permitted to go into British-held territory on condition that he not "give any intelligence to the enemy" and return to Philadelphia. What he wrote and what he did aroused increasing suspicions. He was jailed several times for suspect behavior, and finally permitted to leave for the enemy lines. Even though he was reimbursed by the British government in recognition of his loyalty and zeal for the cause, at war's end he returned to Philadelphia, along with other prominent Loyalists. Despite rumors to the contrary, he had not, unlike his daughter, forsworn his faith. In the records of the Federal District Court in Philadelphia, we have a deposition of his attested to "on the five Books of Moses."

In the tight Jewish communities of New York and Philadelphia, this divided allegiance was most apparent, whereas it was least demonstrable in communities of the deep South. Overall, the evidence suggests that the Jews of Spanish and Portuguese extraction, the long-term residents in the colonies, seem to have been enthusiastic Patriots, while the Ashkenazim were more evenly distributed between Tory and Whig. Most of the Sephardim - merchants like Aaron Lopez, for example - left Newport with the colonial forces, while the Hart and Pollock families of that town remained to work for the British cause, and perhaps suffered more for their decision than any other Jewish families in the colonies. In 1780 the properties of Isaac and Samuel Hart and the latter's son, Samuel, Jr., were confiscated by the Rhode Island Assembly. Moving to Long Island, Isaac Hart fell in defense of an improvised fort which the Loyalists had manned. Rivington's *Gazette* reports that he was "inhumanly fired upon and bayonetted," but the fact is that Hart had forfeited such immunity as might have been due him as a civilian. Jacob and Moses Hart received modest compensation from the British Commissioners of Forfeited Estates.

Closely allied to the Harts and sharing their political views were the Pollocks of Newport. Edmund Burke took up the cause of the Pollocks in an eloquent speech in the Commons, wherein he related that one of the Pollocks had been driven from Rhode Island for importing tea contrary to the nonimportation agreement, and after being forced to flee Long Island, where the British army had turned some lands over to him, he settled in St. Eustatius, there once more suffering substantial losses after the British capture of that Island, on which occasion the whole Jewish community of a hundred persons was rounded up, and each one searched and stripped of his possessions. Ezra Stiles lists seven other Jews who remained behind at Newport after the British occupation, suggesting that their Patriot sympathies were at best lukewarm, and an official list of Newport Tories includes another five known to be Jews.

In New York City the Jewish community was also split. The Congregation Shearith Israel was torn by dissension. The majority of the membership, following the lead of Gershom Mendes Seixas, decided to disband the congregation, and on the arrival of the British forces in the summer of '76 sought refuge in Connecticut or Philadelphia, while the Jewish Tories remained in the city. Others remained not out of choice, but were given little peace. I refer to those resting in the old Jewish cemetery set atop an elevation near Chatham Square on the outskirts of the Patriot fortifications overlooking the East River. While skirmishes were fought on and around the site, the British soldiery removed the lead plates bearing inscriptions and melted them down for ammunition. Very much alive, however, were Jewish supporters of George III like the Hessian soldier Alexander Zuntz, who doubled as commissary for the Hessian general staff and served as president of the rump Jewish congregation. The signatures of some fifteen Jews, some of them relatives of Patriot families like the Myers, Nathans, and

Hayses, signed the ardent Loyalist address presented to Admiral Lord Richard Howe and his brother Sir William on October 16, 1776.

If I have dwelt at some length on the role of Jews as Tories or neutrals, it is merely to put in perspective the assertions of that early proto-Zionist, Mordecai Noah, that his co-religionists had been one hundred percent pro-Revolution. That was a pardonable exaggeration, considering the patriotic antecedents of Noah himself, but the roster of American Jewish participants on the side of the Revolution is so impressive that it is clear that Whiggish Jews constituted an overwhelming majority of the scattered Jewish communities in the thirteen colonies. With the Catholics they stand as an exception to the generalization that the Tories were an aggregation of conscious minorities whose status was threatened by the Revolution. Perhaps because of their involvement with commerce, Jewish protesters against the new British revenue program were proportionately more numerous than those of any other ethnic or religious group.

Even before the formal start of the war, Jewish merchants were prominent in signing the nonimportation agreements, and their role in active military support and in financing, provisioning, and supplying the Continental and state military forces is a conspicuous one. Let us take two examples out of at least a hundred that could be selected. Immediately there comes to mind Francis Salvador.

Elected a member of the South Carolina Assembly, preceded only by Joseph Ottolengui of Georgia as a Jew in a colonial legislature, Salvador also served in his state's first and second Revolutionary Provincial Congresses. He accompanied the Presbyterian evangelist William Tennent into the heart of Tory country in North Carolina to persuade the Loyalists to join the Association. On July 24, 1776, Chief Justice Drayton wrote Salvador: "No news yet from Philadelphia; every ear is turned that way anxiously waiting for the word 'Independence.' I say, 'God speed the passage of it.' 'Amen,' say you." On August 1 Salvador was shot and scalped in an Indian and Tory ambush. Probably he never learned that the American Congress had declared that independence for which he had given his life. As evidence of divisions over the war even in Jewish families, it is worth mentioning that back in England Salvador's brother-in-law, Samuel Prado, was fearful, because of his loyalty to the Crown, that estates which he had never visited in South Carolina had been confiscated, and he filed a claim of loss just to be on the safe side.

Of David Salisbury Franks, history tells us a great a deal. Because he defended the right of a demonstrator to protest against George III - in this case the bust of the king at Montreal was daubed over with the words, "This is the pope of Canada and the fool of England" - Franks was jailed. Once he got out, he sought a more liberal climate, and although he is known to have been president of the Spanish-Portuguese Congregation of Montreal, he removed from that city to Philadelphia in 1775 and enlisted in the Continental army. He became

a major and aide-de-camp to Benedict Arnold. Arnold's treason cast a
shadow over the patriotism of Richard Varick and David Franks,
Arnold's principal aides. Varick was acquitted in a court-martial, and
all charges were dropped against Franks. Indeed, he was sent abroad
with diplomatic dispatches as a mark of Congress's esteem, delivering
to John Jay in Madrid Congress's commission to negotiate the peace.
Promoted to the rank of lieutenant-colonel, he was sent abroad once
more with a copy of the ratification of the Definitive Treaty of Peace.
He served in 1784 as Vice-Consul at Marseilles, and the following year
accompanied the American agent to Morocco to negotiate with that
piratical nation a treaty, which he brought back to the United States
early in 1787. Thus, the Jews and the Arabs got involved with each
other very early.

Salvador and Franks are the best known among the Jewish military figures; but the list of those distinguishing themselves in military
action is impressive. The Southern contingent of Jews in the rebel military forces seems all out of scale with their slender numbers. Almost
the entire adult Jewish male population of Charleston, augmented by
Jews who fled from Georgia, served in Captain Lushington's Company,
which became known as the "Jew Company," a distinction attesting to
the fact that the Jews and non-Jews in the company were about
equally divided. One of those who was to give a good account of himself
under fire was Jacob I. Cohen. Some years later, as a member of the
Richmond firm of Cohen and Isaacs, he hired a frontiersman named
Daniel Boone to survey his land on the Licking River in far-off Kentucky. Enraged at the Patriot activities of the Sheftalls and Philip
Minis, Governor James Wright of Georgia wrote the authorities, in the
course of the war, that the Jewish Whig refugees should not be permitted to return to Georgia and that other Jews should be prevented from
emigrating to the colony. "For these people, my lord, were found to a
man to have been violent rebels and persecutors of the king's loyal
subjects. And however this law may appear at first sight," Wright
insisted, "be assured, my lord, that the times require these exertions
and without which the loyal subjects have no peace or security in the
province." Elsewhere I have likened this advice to the blind panic that
led to the wholesale arrest and incarceration of the Nisei immediately
after Pearl Harbor, a deed which has stained America's record for civil
rights.

Apart from the battlefield, Jews from their connections and exper-
tise in shipping, trade, and finance, made substantial contributions to
the successful operation of the war. The Jewish share of privateering,
to cite one example, is estimated at six percent of the total, a figure far
out of proportion to its slender population, and including the activities
of such prominent figures as Moses Michael Hays of Boston, Isaac
Moses, a partner of Robert Morris in the Black Prince, and the firm of
Moses Levy and Company. A chief victim of privateering depredations
was the great merchant shipper of Newport, Aaron Lopez. At the outbreak of the Revolution he was the owner of thirty vessels engaged in

European and West Indian trade and the whale fisheries. Lopez's espousal of the American cause virtually wrecked his business; nearly all his vessels were lost before the war was over; some of them, according to his memorial to the Continental Congress, had been captured by American privateers, and the Congressional Court of Admiralty and Appeals sustained him in at least one suit.

In the Southern theater of military operations, no Jew played a larger civilian role than Mordecai Sheftall, leader of the Savannah Jewish community, and chairman of the insurgent Committee of Christ Church Parish. He was nominated in 1778 for the post of Deputy Commissary General of Issues to the Continental troops in South Carolina and Georgia and Deputy Commissary General of Purchase and Issues to the militia, but fell into enemy hands before the formal commission could be confirmed by Congress. When the British occupied Savannah in December 1778, Sheftall was captured by a body of Highlanders, transferred to a prison ship, listed as "Chairman Rebel Committee," and regarded as barred thereby from holding a public office in royal Georgia. His claim to reimbursement of advances made as Deputy Commissary General of Issues was rejected by Congress, although persistently pressed. Sheftall's fortune was apparently depleted, if not entirely liquidated, as a result of his war involvements, despite his efforts to recoup his losses by privateering operations after his release from imprisonment. In the Western theater of operations, Simon Nathan advanced large sums for George Rogers Clark's campaign, only to be repaid in worthless Continental paper.

Perhaps no Patriot in the American Revolution boasted a more romantic and seemingly improbable career than Haym Salomon, a Polish immigrant who arrived in New York in 1772 and set himself up as a commission merchant, dealer in securities, and ship broker. He soon struck up a friendship with Alexander McDougall, a leader of the Sons of Liberty, with whom he cast his lot. When, in September 1776, New York City was burned ("whether by Providence or some stout fellow," as George Washington put it), the irate British occupation forces sought scapegoats. Salomon was picked up as a suspect and thrust into jail, probably the Old Sugar House located on what is now Liberty Street. Owing to his fluency in German as well as in five other languages, the British found him useful in communicating with the Hessians, who numbered about half the occupation troops. Because of these services, he was released from jail and permitted to resume his business activities. Whether or not he continued to use his military contacts to have access to prisons or prison ships, it seems clear that Salomon was soon involved in underground activities to help American prisoners of war escape. With the evacuation of Philadelphia and the rebuff at Monmouth, the British in New York became panicky. Salomon was arrested in early August 1778, and jailed this time on suspicion of espionage and sabotage. Sentenced to death in a drumhead court-martial, Salomon effected a miraculous escape with the aid of his friend McDougall, now a Patriot general. On August 25, 1778, we find him in Philadelphia, petitioning Congress that his war activities had cost him all his effects and credit to the amount of five or six thousand pounds sterling.

In Philadelphia, Salomon was picked by the Chevalier de La Luzerne, the French minister to Congress, to serve as paymaster-general of the French forces in America. At his brokerage office in Front Street, feverish financial activities were carried on. It was only natural that when, in February 1781, Congress named Robert Morris to be Superintendent of Finance, virtually endowing him with the powers of a financial dictator, Morris should lean on Salomon. The latter had already advanced the government considerable sums of money on the dubious security it offered because, as we know, the federal government had gone bankrupt in its efforts to finance the war. Now, with his own personal endorsement, Salomon sold Morris's bills of exchange, providing much of the funds that kept the government in motion, and charging only one-fourth of one percent commission, perhaps a third of the going rate. In the three-year period of Morris's Superintendency of Finance, Salomon had no less than seventy-five transactions with Morris, advancing in hard currency over $200,000.

The later career of Salomon proved tragic. With the war's end, Salomon planned to move his operations back to New York, but the transfer was never affected. His health seriously impaired as a result of his wartime imprisonment by the British, he died at the age of forty-five. The Revolution had not enriched him. His total assets amounted to $44,732; his debts to $45,292. His estate was insolvent by $560. Had the liquidation of his estate not been forced, the loan office, treasury, and state certificates that Salomon's estate held, to the extent of over $150,000, would have been redeemed at par when Alexander Hamilton became Secretary of the Treasury - a fact nobody knew in 1785, and all the Salomon family would have suffered would have been a loss on the worthless Continental currency. Thus Salomon, who had lost two fortunes in the course of the Revolutionary War, had risked his property and pledged his credit on behalf of the Revolutionary Congress when a crisis of confidence existed.

In short, from Aaron Lopez to Mordecai Sheftall to Haym Salomon, every single conspicuous Jewish figure who was involved in financing or supplying the Continental forces ended up broke.

If the American Revolution proved to be a liberating movement for various minorities, including the Jews, there were moments when Jews in America felt that they were being singled out for discrimination. Both sides in the Revolution required the inhabitants to take loyalty oaths. One of the earliest oaths of loyalty to the Revolutionary cause was that exacted by the Rhode Island Assembly in June 1775, of male inhabitants over sixteen years of age "suspected of being inimical to the United American Colonies." The officers of the Rhode Island brigade soon listed seventy-seven inhabitants of Newport suspected of "inimical" views, among them three known Jewish Tories and Moses M.

Hays. When four members of the General Assembly tendered the test to the Newport suspects, Isaac Hart refused to sign the test until it was required from all alike; Myer Pollock declined on the ground that it was "contrary to the custom of Jews," but Moses Michael Hays, who in fact was no Tory, refused on more elaborate grounds. He demanded that his accusers come forward and asked that the accusation be read, which was done. Although avowing "the strongest principles and attachments to the just rights and privileges of this my native land" and his support for the war as a "just" one, he declined to subscribe, first, because the burden of proof of his inimical status rested on his accusers; secondly, because as a Jew he was not allowed to vote, contrary to the state's constitution; thirdly, because the test was "not general," and finally because neither the Continental Congress nor the state assembly had ever singled out "in this contest . . . the society of Israelites to which I belong." He followed up this refusal with a petition to the General Assembly avowing his attachment to the Patriot cause and insisting upon "the rights and privileges due other free citizens." So far as the records disclose, this ended the controversy.

If there is an overtone of anti-Semitism in this incident, or a forecast of the McCarthyism of the 1950s, it in no wise reflects the climate of opinion prevailing in the American colonies on the verge of rebellion. When one considers that the American Revolution was a civil war, that leading Patriots held a deep and abiding prejudice against Roman Catholics, that the rhetoric of abuse in which both sides indulged has seldom been surpassed except in our own time, and, further, that the Jews seemed especially vulnerable since they provided scapegoats on both sides of the conflict, it is astonishing how little anti-Semitism was stirred up in America as a result of the Revolutionary crisis. Contrariwise, prejudice and animosity toward Jews was widespread in contemporary England. Jews were humiliated and physically attacked on the streets, which resounded to the tunes of anti-Jewish ballads, anti-Semitism was a part of the religious indoctrination of the High Church, and the prominence of Jews in finance was reflected in the frequent caricatures of the Jew as a moneylender. One of the most celebrated of Gillray's caricatures depicts the Earl of Shelburne, with a booted and spurred French courier on his left just arrived from Paris, bearing news that the Preliminaries had been signed with America on November 30, 1782, and on his right a group of Jewish moneylenders waiting to receive payment of sums allegedly advanced on the security of the Shelburne House and about to be paid off with the fruits of stock manipulation. The conversion of the eccentric Lord George Gordon to Judaism hardly cooled latent English anti-Semitism. Nor did Lord George's proposal, dated barely a month before the signing of the Definitive Peace with America and addressed to Elias Lindo and Nathan Salomons on behalf of the Portuguese and German Jews respectively. On the verge of conversion, the irrepressible peer proposed that Jews could stop the war by withholding credits. It was the playwright-diplomat Richard Cumberland who, single-handedly, stepped into the breach, and through his periodical, *The Observer* and his play *The Jew* sought to correct the current image in England of the Jew as rogue, usurer, or buffoon.

Unlike England, the tie-in of Jews with usury and sharp financial dealings was rarely made in America of Revolutionary times, although isolated instances may be found. One Loyalist who sought to exploit the traditional view of the Jewish usurer was Miers Fisher, a Quaker lawyer and former Tory exile, who, on his return to Philadelphia at the end of the war, sought to obtain a charter for the Bank of Pennsylvania, a potential competitor of Robert Morris's Bank of North America. He contended that the chartering of his bank would reduce the rate of interest, thus protecting the people against the exactions of the Jewish brokers. Not only was this a diversionary maneuver by which Tories attempted to exonerate themselves by inciting prejudice against Jews, but it was an implied attack on Robert Morris and his bank, which had received strong support from Jews. A "Jew Broker," the pseudonym believed to have been used in this case by Haym Salomon, sent a scorching reply to the press. Denouncing the aspersions "cast so indiscriminately on the Jews of this city at large," the writer not only accused Fisher of libeling the Jews but of injuring that liberty of conscience which the Jews enjoyed. Defending the Jews as having been "early uniform, decisive Whigs," and "second to none" in their "patriotism and attachment" to their country, he insisted on the injustice of denigrating an entire group "for the faults of a few."

This exchange must be put down as exceptional. Anti-Semitism was definitely out of fashion in the America of the Revolutionary era. When Ezra Stiles reported that in May 1773 Governor Wanton of Rhode Island, together with Judges Oliver and Auchmuty, sat with the president of the congregation at a Jewish religious service held at the Newport synagogue, he was very casually reporting an event which would have been impossible to parallel in Europe at that time. When, in 1809, John Adams, taking exception to the anti-Semitism of Bolingbroke and Voltaire, insisted that "the Hebrews have done more to civilize men than any other nation," he was merely voicing sentiments that President Washington, perhaps less effusively had placed on the records a good deal earlier. I need hardly add that John Adams was expressing his affection for the people of the book, not for contemporary Jewry. Behind the effusive acknowledgment of affirmative Jewish qualities lurked a hope on the part of Hebraists like Ezra Stiles of Yale that someday the Jews would see the light and unite with Christians in accepting the religion of the majority.

Having reviewed the individual experience of the more conspicuous Jewish figures in the American Revolution, it is now fitting that we should consider the role played by the scattered Jewish communities and community leaders in acting, along with other minority groups, as a catalyst to quicken demands for equal rights and civil liberties. Just as the Catholics played a decisive role in the passage of the Maryland

Toleration Act of 1649 to reassure Protestant settlers, and the Baptists sparked the passage of Virginia's revolutionary legislation for religious liberty, so, too, the Jews had, from the beginning of their settlement in America, fought Director-General Stuyvesant in New Netherland to win the basic right of settlement, economic privileges, the right of public worship, and various political rights. The fact that the Jews back in the seventeenth century had waged the battle of other minority groups as well as their own is clear from Stuyvesant's warning to the Dutch West India Company. "Giving them liberty," he declared, "we cannot refuse the Lutherans and the Papists."

Was the Jew in America an alien? The issue was raised not many years after the passage of the Navigation Act of 1660, which barred aliens from the colonial trade, and a draft of the Act of 1696, which by its phrasing seemed to bar Jews who had succeeded in obtaining naturalization in the colonies. The Jewish traders petitioned the government, asserting that "those of the Hebrew Nation do look upon what ever Countrey they retire" to "as their native country." The Jews were supported by a similar representation from a group of French Huguenots acting in behalf of their co-religionists in Carolina and New York. As finally enacted, the statute of 1696 omitted the objectionable provision, an omission which was a resounding victory for minority groups both in England and the colonies.

By the time of the American Revolution Jews had achieved civil rights and rights of worship, but their political position was by no means clarified. In 1737 New York disqualified the winner of an election to the legislature because Jews had voted for him. The legislature was persuaded by the contention of a New York attorney of prominence, William Smith, who pointed out that Jews were disqualified from voting in English Law, and to clinch his case he reminded his hearers of the guilt the Jews allegedly bore for the Crucifixion. In Rhode Island the Superior Court held that no Jews could hold any office or vote in choosing others - this in the plantation found by Roger Williams!

Considering the fact that the Jews in America enjoyed civil rights long before they were accorded them in England, and that the great campaign for the admission of Jews to the British Parliament was not secured until 1858, it is not surprising that some American states proved dilatory about letting down political barriers to such minorities as Catholics, Jews, Deists, or nonbelievers. Even states like Virginia, which acted boldly in providing for religious freedom, did not at once remove political discrimination against various minorities. The great exception was the New York State Constitution, whose two-hundredth anniversary was appropriately commemorated on April 20, 1977. That constitution, which imposed on the Jews no disabilities whatsoever, justified the encomiums of contemporary New York leaders of being "wisely framed to preserve the inestimable blessings of civil and religious liberty," and may well be, as one American Jewish historian claims, "the first emancipatory law in modern history."

New York's example heartened religious minorities and the friends of religious liberty in other states, notably in Pennsylvania, where an unusually democratic constitution guaranteed freedom of worship, but at the same time fixed a religious test for office-holding, one which effectively barred Jews. Early in 1784 a group of Jewish leaders of the Philadelphia synagogue, including their "rabbi," Gershom Seixas, their president, Simon Nathan, and the associates of their council - Asher Myers, Bernard Gratz, and Haym Salomon - petitioned the Pennsylvania Council of Censors "in behalf of themselves and their brethren Jews, residing in Pennsylvania." They protested the tenth section of the state constitution, requiring members of the assembly to subscribe to a declaration which ended in these words: "I do acknowledge the Scriptures of the old and new Testament to be given by divine inspriation." Very properly the memorialists pointed out that this clause violated the second paragraph of the state's declaration of rights, asserting "that no man who acknowledges the being of a God can be justly deprived or abridged of any civil rights as a citizen on account of his religious sentiments." The point was made that the disability of Jews to serve in the assembly might impel Jewish immigrants to go to New York or to such other places in the United States where no such discrimination prevailed. While disavowing strong political ambitions, the memorialists denounced the exclusion test as "a stigma upon their nation and their religion," particularly undeserved in view of the Patriot contribution of the Jews to the cause of the Revolution and their losses suffered as a result of their participation. While the memorial was tabled at that time, Pennsylvania in its new constitution of 1790 removed the New Testament reference, which had in effect excluded Jews from public office.

In addition to Pennsylvania, various other states, following New York's example and Virginia's Notable Act for Religious Freedom of 1785, removed political restrictions against the Jews. Georgia acted in 1789; South Carolina did so simultaneously with Pennsylvania; Delaware removed the bars in 1792; and Vermont a year later. Still other states were slower to respond to Enlightenment currents. For example, the disqualification in the Maryland Constitution of 1776 barring Jews from public office was not removed until 1825. Rhode Island did not secure equal rights for the Jews until the adoption of its constitution in 1842, and North Carolina not until 1868.

If Jews contributed to making the Revolution both a war for independence and a broad movement for change and reform, still they and other religious minorities were beneficiaries of the movement in the original thirteen states to guarantee religious liberty, separate church and state, and drop the religious bars to public office-holding. But it was the federal government rather than the states which provided the most vigorous impetus to the movement. On July 13, 1787, the Congress of the Confederation, meeting in New York City, enacted the Northwest Territory Ordinance, whose first article ordained that "no person, demeaning himself in a peaceable and orderly manner, shall ever be molested on account of his mode of worship, or religious sentiments, in the said territory."

Would the Federal Convention meeting simultaneously in Philadelphia adopt so liberal a stance? Since its sessions were secret, nothing was known to the public of what had been decided prior to the adjournment of the Convention. On August 20, Charles Cotesworth Pinckney had submitted to the Convention, for reference to the Committee on Detail, a number of propositions, among them: "No religious test or qualification shall ever be annexed to any oath of office under authority of the United States." This proposition was referred to the Committee on Detail without debate or further consideration. When the Committee reported back on August 30, Pinckney then moved to amend the article with the addition of these words: "but no religious test shall ever be required as a qualification to any office or public trust under the authority of the United States." Roger Sherman thought the clause unnecessary, "the prevailing liberality being a sufficient security against such tests." But Gouverneur Morris and General Pinckney approved the motion, which was agreed to unanimously. The entire article was adopted, with only North Carolina voting no and Maryland divided.

Not knowing what had transpired, Jonas Phillips, a long-time patriot of New York, who had removed to Philadelphia before the start of hostilities and served in the Philadelphia militia, memorialized the convention on September 7, which he carefully described as "24th Ellul 5547." Using arguments similar to those the synagogue leaders of his city advanced to the Pennsylvania Council of Censors in 1784 in arguing against the test oath, Phillips urged that, should the Convention omit the phrase regarding the divine inspiration of the New Testament, "then the Israelites will think themselves happy to live under a government where all religious societies are on an equal footing." Jonas Phillips appears to have been unduly concerned. In its final form, Article VI of the Federal Constitution requires all federal and state officials to take an oath or affirmation to support the Constitution, with the proviso "but no religious Test shall ever be required as a qualification to any office or public trust under the United States." Finally, of course, one should mention the first article of the Bill of Rights, forbidding Congress to make any law respecting an establishment of religion or prohibiting the free exercise thereof.

It was only fitting that Jews should publicly express their rejoicing when the Constitution was ratified, and Jews joined in public celebrations with their fellow Americans. In Philadelphia their sensibilities were observed by providing for them a special kosher table. Quite properly could Washington applaud the "enlarged and liberal policy" of the new nation, in which "all possess alike liberty of conscience and immunities of citizenship." Significantly, the new President extolled the example of the new nation "which gives to bigotry no sanction, to persecution, no assistance," as "a policy worthy of imitation," lifting the eloquent phrasing from a memorial to him from Yeshuat Israel Congregation of Newport. Or, as he phrased it in a communication to the members of the New Church in Baltimore: "In the enlightened Age and in this land of equal liberty it is our boast, that a man's religious tenets will not forfeit the protection of the Laws, nor deprive him of the right of attaining and holding the highest Offices that are known in the United States."

On this point Washington proved an optimist, because while a Catholic has attained the Presidency, to date the very highest office in the land still eludes non-Christians.

In sum, there is abundant evidence not only from the Revolutionary era but from the whole century of a Jewish presence in America preceding it, to demonstrate that where the Jews gained the equal protection of the laws other minorities were likely to profit thereby, and, further, that the struggles of Presbyterian minorities or French Huguenot minorities or German Pietist minorities or Baptist minorities or Catholic minorities were inseparably tied to the security of the Jewish community. After all, had there been no minority groups in this country, colonial and early national America would have been quite differently structured and doubtless less vital and democratic than the emerging nation proved to be in fact. At least forty percent of the population of the American colonies was of non-English stock, and the followers of the Church of England, though that church was established in a number of colonies, were in fact a numerical minority themselves. Accordingly, toleration and equal rights were the keys to effective functioning of government. Without them discord and civil strife would have stifled opportunity, discouraged immigration, and even have caused a breakdown of law enforcement.

America's toleration toward Jews and other religious minorities, and the steps taken to guarantee their civil and political rights, served as a spur to the movement on the European continent for the emancipation of the Jews, so long victims of discriminatory laws. In their petition to the French National Assembly of January 1790, the Jews of France pointed to America, citing that Revolutionary land for having "rejected the word toleration from its code," for, they cogently reasoned, "to tolerate is, in fact, to suffer that which you could, if you wished, prevent and prohibit." In Western Europe the emancipation of the Jews was finally achieved by the French Revolution and the Code Napoleon. Moses Mendelssohn, that foremost spokesman for Jewish emancipation, and a grand product of the *Aufklarung*, was so stirred by the secular spirit evoked by America's War of Independence that he wrote a new foreword to an older work, using the American Revolution as a pretext to set forth his ideas on the separation of church and state.

Thus, a great world leader in the movement of Jewish emancipation took heart from the grand events on this side of the Atlantic, events in which the voice of the Jews had been raised on numberless occasions on behalf of religious liberty, in opposition to political discrimination, and in support of civil rights for all, and would continue to be raised in the years ahead down to our own time.

A final point. The people of the "Hebrew nation," or "Israelites," as they chose to style themselves, made every effort to join the mainstream of American life. Some assimilated so completely that even the most skilled genealogist cannot trace their descendants. Others, probably a majority of that Revolutionary generation, saw no difficulty in maintaining their identification with Judaism while regarding themselves as Americans on an equality with their non-Jewish associates. With Washington, they recognized the need to develop a "national character," with Hamilton, the vision to "think continentally." Without renouncing their faith, they were quite prepared to be "Americanized," to use a term first coined by John Jay in 1797.

Indeed, the early role of the Jew in America should be borne in mind at a time when notions of cultural pluralism have portrayed society as a collection of minorities and given priority to minority concerns over collective interests. Pushed to extremes, pluralism has spawned separatist Quebec, a tragic bomb-wracked Northern Ireland, Scottish, and Welsh separatism, not to speak of rising bilingualism in some regions of the United States, with its disunifying implications, and the reality of ethnic politics to which every American politician pays obeisance.

The belief that all the varied groups in America could co-exist in a kind of natural harmony was a theory advanced a half-century ago by Horace Kallen, an early and active Zionist. Since then ethnicity in America, from university curricula to popular culture, has assumed directions that might well have given even a Kallen pause. Where pluralism denotes a theory of culture, I would embrace it, especially for its appropriateness to minorities like the Jews, who wish to preserve their religious identity and their blood ties to Israel, and are not likely to forget the rise of Nazism, the Holocaust, and the coercion under which Jews now live in totalitarian states. Where pluralism denotes a theory of power, I confess to grave misgivings. Ethnic pluralism as a basis of power immobilizes government and erodes the national purpose. Most plural societies are either tyrannized by one of the constituent groups or operate under constant instability, thereby posing a threat to the continued functioning of democratic institutions.

In the third century of our national existence, as I see it, our tasks as American Jews steadfast to the traditions of the American Jewish past are, first, to cherish our distinctive cultural values. Irving Howe's brilliant analysis of the process of Americanizing the Jewish immigrant has shown how greatly Jewish ethical and cultural values, traditions, and even personality traits have spurred that growing awareness in the larger community of intellectual values and the need for social reform, while at the same time contributing so much to Jewish self-discovery. To maintain our own cultural values constitutes by itself an enormous challenge in a society where family ties are disintegrating and swift technological change is homogenizing our life and culture without rendering either more homogeneous or more enriching.

We Jews have another task before us, as I see it. While maintaining our respect for diversity, we should take the lead in marking out those political and cultural values and bases of creativity which served to bind together all Americans in achieving a common purpose, consistent with our democratic traditions and the image of America as an "asylum for liberty," a common purpose that will lift our sights and unite us, one that will inspire us with the kind of dedication that impelled Jews and other minorities of Revolutionary days to sacrifice life and treasure for a noble cause.

SOURCE: Gladys Rosen (ed.), *Jewish Life in America: Historical Perspectives* (New York: Ktav, 1978), pp. 8-27. Reprinted by permission of the American Jewish Committee.

CHAPTER II

CHOOSING SIDES IN THE STRUGGLE

The coming of the Revolution confronted American Jews with a dilemma. Like many of their non-Jewish neighbors, they had greatly benefited from British rule, some maintaining close personal and economic ties with the Mother Country. Yet no less than other Americans, Jews felt aggrieved at British colonial policies. In the pre-war decades, some Jews participated in the nonimportation agreements and boycotted British goods. Others prayed for peace, hoping that King George would change his ways and accede to colonists' demands. Individually, Jews based their decisions largely on business, national and personal considerations. Many vacillated and pledged allegiance to both sides in the dispute for as long as they could. But when finally forced to choose, only a minority of Jews sided wholeheartedly with the Crown. Most came down on the side of the Whigs and cast their lot for independence.

THE AGONY OF AARON LOPEZ

Stanley F. Chyet

*Stanley Chyet presents here a moving account of how Aaron Lopez
agonized over which side to support in the Revolutionary struggle; Lopez
(1731-1782), a leading merchant in Newport, Rhode Island, fled his home
soon after the Revolution broke out. After living in Portsmouth, Providence and Boston, he finally settled down with other Newport Jews in
Leicester, Massachusetts.*

During all the years of disturbance leading up to the final rupture
in 1776, Aaron Lopez, it is clear, had been something less than
unwavering in his support of the Continental cause. Fugitive that he
was from an Inquisition-ridden Portugal, able in British-ruled America
to practice his religion without fear, permitted under the aegis of the
British crown to pursue his commercial affairs with as much opportunity as was accorded any other enterprising colonial merchant, Aaron
did not see in George III the royal brute that Thomas Paine perceived.
When we find him complaining to Wright in March 1775 that "our
sanguine [had he in mind their expectations or their belligerence?] Sons
of Liberty [had] debarr'd us from an importation of English goods," or
when he "fervently invoke[s God's] mercies and pray[s] for our preservation from the impending calamities that at present seems to
threaten this infatuated meridian," we cannot think that revolution
had much appeal for him. And something more may have been
involved. Aaron never expressed it in so many words - none at least
that have survived - but the European in him must have been put to a
grievous test by the imminence of revolution. He had devoted years of
his life to the practical effort of Europeanizing his American surround-
ings, bringing to America in profusion not only the goods, but equally
the amenities of European life. It is unlikely that he ever conceived of
his work in any such light, but the effect of his strivings - and indeed
the strivings of every merchant-shipper - was to recreate America in
the image of Europe. And now, faced with the prospect of an America
cut free from the greatest of European empires, how could he find it in
himself to respond with enthusiasm? It would be saying too much to
suggest that he ever thought this out systematically. There is no evidence that he did, and in the end he would not resist the forces which
were bent on secession. Ultimately he could not be indifferent to the
dream of independence, but it seems undeniable that given his preference, he would have made haste slowly, very slowly, towards denying
the crown of England.

Still, as every hope of peace vanished that year of 1776, Aaron
appears to have made a choice. He would not forsake the country

whose hospitality he had enjoyed for more than twenty years, and no longer would King George have a claim on his loyalty. That the passions of an ardent rebel were quite remote from his decision is suggested by a letter Wright addressed to him from Jamaica a year later, in June 1777. "My dear friend," wrote Captain Wright,

> happy am I to find yo are still on this side your grave, altho' deeply affected with the unnatural reverse of days. I sincerely condole with yo on the melancholly situation of that once happy country [America], and readily admit there is no real happiness to be expected in this frail world whose vicessitudes, as yo very justly observe, must be encountered with a becoming resignation.

Years later, when British losses at Cowpens, South Carolina, and Lord Cornwallis' Yorktown debacle promised an early end to the war, Aaron could rejoice over "our glorious conquest of Virginia and the signal late victory gained by our brave troops at South Carolina both which happy events cannot but presage much felicity to this continent." In the mid-1770s, however, it was no hot revolutionary ardor, it was a becoming resignation in the face of a bitter situation that led Aaron to cast his lot with the seceding colonies.

SOURCE: Stanley F. Chyet, *Lopez of Newport* (Detroit, 1970), pp. 155-156. Reprinted by permission of Wayne State University Press.

1. Mordecai Sheftall: Revolutionary Leader - 1775

Mordecai Sheftall (1735-1797) was one of the leaders of the Revolutionary movement in Georgia and chairman of the rebel committee which prior to the outbreak of war enforced the boycott of British goods. Associated with Sheftall was another Jew, Philip Minis (1733-1789). Interesting, the ship Clarissa, *referred to in this document, was owned by Aaron Lopez of Newport, who suffered a considerable monetary loss due to his co-religionist's revolutionary ardor.*

The deposition of Richard Bissell, master of the ship *Clarissa*, belonging to Rhode Island, but now lying in Savannah River, taken on oath the 12th day of September, 1775, before the Honourable Anthony Stokes, barrister at law, Chief Justice of the said provence.

This deponent, being duly sworn on the Holy Evangelists of Almighty God, maketh oath and saith:

That he arrived in this province on or about the twenty fifth day of July last, from the island of Jamaica, having on board the said ship ten hogs heads of melasses, and sundry other goods;

That this deponent, about the middle of August, advertized the said melasses for public sale; that soon after the said advertizement appeared, one Stephen Biddurph, messenger to the Parochial Committee in Savannah (as this deponent has been informed and verily believes), came to this deponent and told him that the committee ordered him to appear before them;

That when this deponent went before the said committee, he there saw sitting in the chair one Mordecai Sheftal, of Savannah, Minis, of Savannah, both which persons profess the Jewish religion; one Platt who acts as secretary to the said committee, one Lyons of Savannah, blacksmith, one Tondee of Savannah, tavern keeper, and several others, whose names this deponent doth not know;

That the said Mordecai Sheftal told this deponent that the aforesaid melasses could not be landed in this provence and that they must be carried back to Jamacai or abide by the consequences;

That this deponent hath since been obliged to sign a bond, at the Custom House, for the delivery of the said melasses at the island of Jamaica aforesaid.

                                        Richard Bissell
Sworn the day and year aforesaid: Anthony Stokes

A true copy: Preston & Pryce

2. A Prayer for Peace - 1776

This prayer, probably composed by Reverend Gershom Seixas, was recited at a special service held at Congregation Shearith Israel of New York on the "day of humiliation, fasting and prayer" called by the Second Continental Congress in 1776. Once independence was declared, Seixas along with many of his congregants, sided with the Whigs and left New York in advance of the oncoming British troops.

O Lord: the God of our Fathers Abraham, Isaac and Jacob, may it please thee, to put it in the heart of our Sovereign Lord, George the third, and in the hearts of his Councellors, Princes and Servants, to turn away their fierce Wrath from against North America. And to destroy the wicked devices of our enemies, that it may fall on their own heads. That there may no more blood be shed in these Countries, O Lord our God, we beseech thee to open unto us the gates of mercy on this our solemn Fast. And that our prayers and the prayers of all the people that stand before thee this day, may come before thee that the [MS. torn] may no more pass through our Land. And that thou mayest send the Angels of mercy to proclaim Peace to all America and to the inhabetants thereof. That thou mayest once more plant an everlasting peace between Great Britain and her Colonies as in former times and confirm unto us what is written. And they shall beat their swords into Plow-shares, and their spears into pruning hooks; Nation shall not lift up sword against Nation, neither shall they learn war any more. Amen.

3. The Strains of Independence in Newport - 1776

Newport merchant Moses M. Hays (1739-1805), though in partner-ship with one pro-British Jewish loyalist, Myer Polock, and brother-in-law of another, Isaac Touro, signed this declaration of loyalty to the Revolutionary cause as demanded by the Rhode Island Assembly in June 1776. A month later, following the Declaration of Independence, the Assembly summoned him to sign an additional declaration of loyalty, one demanded only of those suspected of being "enemical to the United Colonies in America." This time, Hays refused to sign, for reasons spelled out in Document 4. He nevertheless remained loyal to the Whig cause and subsequently moved to Boston where he became a successful businessman and a prominent community figure.

We, the subscribers, do solemnly and sincerely declare that we believe the war resistance and opposition in which the United Ameri-can Colonies are now engaged against the fleets and armies of Great Britain is on the part of said colonies just and necessary and that we will not directly nor indirectly afford assistance of any sort or kind whatsoever to the said fleet and armies during the continuance of the present war, but that we will heartily assist in the defense of the United Colonies.

1776, June, Session of Assembly, M.M. Hayes

4. Moses M. Hays Stands On His Rights - 1776

In refusing to sign a special loyalty oath, in addition to the general one to which he had already subscribed (Document 3), Moses M. Hays implied that the motives of his accusers were impure, and that he was being suspected in part because he was a Jew. In a letter to the Rhode Island General Assembly, however, he was more contrite: "I ask of your Honors the rights and privileges due other free citizens when I conform to everything done and acted, and again implore that the justice of your Honors may interfer[e] in my behalf . . . that I may have an oppert[unit]'y of vindication before your Honors."

He refused to sign the test and called for his accusers. He was then told there was a number present whom he there saw. He likewise called for his accusation which was read. I have and ever shall hold the strongest principles and attachments to the just rights and privileges of this my native land, and ever have and shall conform to the rules and acts of this government and pay, as I always have, my proportion of its exigencies. I always have asserted my sentiments in favor of America and confess the war on its part just. I decline subscribing the test at present from these principles:

First, that I deny ever being inimical to my country and call for my accusers and proof of conviction,

Second, that I am an Israelite and am not allowed the liberty of a vote or voice in common with the rest of the voters, though consistent with the constitution, and the other colonies,

Thirdly, because the test is not general and consequently subject to many glaring inconveniences,

Fourthly, Continental Congress nor the General Assembly of this nor the legislatures of the other colonies have never in this contest taken any notice or countenance respecting the society of Israelites to which I belong. When any rule order or directions is made by the Congress or General Assembly I shall to the utmost of my power adhere to the same.

5. Benjamin Levy Offers Hospitality to Robert Morris - 1776

This letter from Benjamin Levy to Robert Morris provides an example of staunch Jewish pro-Whig sentiment. Levy (1726-1802), a notable Baltimore merchant, offered to open his home to his friend, Morris, then a member of the Continental Congress, in the dark days preceding the fall of Philadelphia. Later, Levy helped raise funds for the new government.

My dear Morris:

It is said that if the Congress are oblig'd to leave Philadelphia, they intend coming to this town. We have two very good rooms on our first floor upstairs, which we purpose for you and Mrs. Morris. We have one spare bed, our house is good and large, and think if you can be supply'd with bedding from Mr. Aquilla Hall, who is but about 25 miles from hence, we could accommodate all your children and three or four servants, having other apartments that will do exceeding well. But sincerely pray that you may not be under the necessity of leaving your home and that we shall soon hear of the enemy retireing. As these are not times for compliments and ceremony, I need not give you assurances of making you welcome as I ever profess'd myself,

Your truly affectionate humb. ser[an]'t,
Benjamin Levy

Rachel [my wife] joins me in compliments to Mrs. Morris.
Baltimore, Friday 13 Decb'r, 1776.

6. The Sad Fate of the Loyalist Polocks - 1781

*This document recounts the fate of the Polocks, a prominent family
of Newport Jewish loyalists. Myer Polock (see Document 3) had his estate
confiscated. His brother-in-law, Isaac Hart, was bayoneted and clubbed to
death. The rest of the family suffered grievously. Edmund Burke, the
great British statesman, used the Polock story to buttress his case for a
compensation act. Burke's speech, from which the excerpt printed here is
taken, was delivered in the House of Commons on May 14, 1781.*

Two more Jews had been detected also in a breach of the order for
delivering up all their money. Upon one of them were found 900
Johannes. This poor man's case was peculiarly severe; his name was
Pollock. He had formerly lived on Rhode Island; and because he had
imported tea contrary to the command of the Americans, he was
stripped of all he was worth and driven out of the island; his brother
shared in his misfortunes, but did not survive them; his death
increased the cares of the survivor, as he got an additional family, in
his brother's children, to provide for. Another Jew married his sister;
and both of them, following the British army, had for their loyalty
some lands given them, along with some other American refugees, on
Long Island, by Sr. William Howe: they built a kind of fort there to
defend themselves; but it was soon after attacked and carried by the
Americans, and not a man who defended it escaped either death or
captivity; the Jew's brother-in-law fell during the attack; he survived;
and had then the family of his deceased brother and brother-in-law, his
mother and sister, to support; he settled at St. Eustasius where he
maintained his numerous family, and had made some money, when he
and his family were once more ruined, by the commanders of a British
force, to whose cause he was so attached; and in whose cause he had
lost two brothers, and his property twice.

CHAPTER III

JEWS AND THE WAR EXPERIENCE

The Jewish experience of the Revolutionary War generally mirrored that of the rest of the population. As we have seen, Jews displayed divided allegiances, although the majority aligned themselves with the patriotic Whigs. Jews in the war fought as soldiers and officers, functioned as financiers, privateers, and suppliers, and in a few cases won special notice for their activities. Like other colonists, they also suffered the various travails of war: death, injury, exile, relocation, and total financial ruin.

These similarities notwithstanding, the Jewish experience did nonetheless differ from that of the mainstream in several important particulars. First, Jews were a numerically insignificant minority group, 1500 to 2000 out of a total population of 2,500,000. They enjoyed civic rights but not political equality, which helps explain why they did not contribute political or intellectual leaders to either side in the struggle. In addition, perhaps because of their extensive commercial involvements and demographic profile, Jews participated in protests against British economic policies more frequently, proportionately speaking, than did members of other minority groups. Their share of privateering during the war, for example, estimated at 6%, far exceeded their share in the population. Finally, Jews in the Revolutionary era periodically found themselves singled out as Jews. Most of the time no malicious intent was involved; it was just that Jews were perceived as different. But occasionally more serious incidents did occur, and in such cases, Jews generally responded vigorously.

JEWS AND THE WAR EFFORT

Jacob R. Marcus

Jacob R. Marcus underscores here the difficulty, on the one hand, of evaluating Jews' role in the military fight for independence, and on the other hand, the ease with which their role in securing the financial well-being of the nation can be gauged. He sets forth available evidence, and concludes that "the real Jewish contribution to the war effort" lay in the Jews' ability to keep commodities flowing.

David Salisbury Franks was an American who had moved to Canada, the fourteenth colony. When General Richard Montgomery took Montreal from the English, the civilian Franks lent the troops money, sold them supplies, and advanced them funds when there was a farthing in the military chest. Looked upon by the British as one of the principal leaders of sedition, Franks had to flee with the American forces when they were driven out. He joined them as a volunteer, remained in the service throughout the war, and rose to the rank of lieutenant colonel.

An even more enthusiastic patriot was Franks's fellow Pennsylvanian Solomon Bush, who became a kinsman of Mordecai Sheftall when Sheftall's son Moses married Bush's sister Nelly. Young Solomon Bush joined the army in the early days because he wanted to "revenge the rongs of my injured country." He soon rose to the rank of deputy adjutant general of the state militia. Severely wounded in a battle near Philadelphia, he was carried to his father's home till betrayed to the British by a "villain." The English were kind enough to parole the wounded officer, but while receiving medical treatment from them, he discovered that a spy had infiltrated Washington's headquarters. Bush lost as little time as he could in alerting the Whigs.

Isaac Franks, a Whig member of this widespread Anglo-American clan, became a lieutenant colonel in the Pennsylvania militia, but that was after the war. In 1776, at the age of seventeen, he enlisted in a regiment of volunteers, arming and equipping himself at his own expense. After the Battle of Long Island, when his company retreated to New York City, he was captured by the British and thrown into prison. Three months later this daring youngster escaped in the dead of winter, crossing the Hudson in a leaky skiff with only one paddle. Arriving on the Jersey shore, he rejoined the American forces and remained in the service until 1782. For most of these years he was a forage master and a noncommissioned quartermaster in and about West Point. The highest rank he reached during the Revolution was that of ensign in a Massachusetts regiment. After six years of practically continuous service with the Continentals, this veteran retired at the ripe age of twenty-three and went into business in Philadelphia. Achieving a modest degree of success, he bought the Deshler House in Germantown. During the war this attractive home had served the British briefly as army headquarters; in 1793, during the yellow fever epidemic, Franks rented the place furnished to President Washington. After the scourge had abated and the President had vacated the mansion, Washington could not fail to notice as he scrutinized his bill that Ensign Franks had charged for six missing items: one flatiron, one large fork, and four platters.

How many Jews served in the militia and in the Continental line? That will never be known, no matter how carefully one checks the records in the National Archives. Combing the lists will indeed bring to light the names of Cohens, Levis, Moseses, and Solomonses. Some of these men were born Christians; Joseph Smith was not. After enlisting in the Third Maryland Regiment at the age of twenty-three, Smith saw service in Pennsylvania, the Jerseys, and the South. Wounded at Camden, South Carolina, in 1780, he fell into British hands and remained a prisoner until he returned home to Baltimore. In signing the company payroll, he made his mark. When he applied for a pension after the war, it developed that Smith's real name was Elias Pollock; he could write, but the only script he employed was the Hebrew. Why had he concealed his name? He may well have been a runaway debtor seeking to escape imprisonment; he may have been an indentured servant or a Maryland "transport," a criminal serving out his term in the colonies. Or the simple answer may be that, fearing prejudice, he adopted the innocuous Anglo-Saxon "Smith" to conceal his Jewish origin.

Though not a soldier, still another member of the Franks clan rendered a great service to the new Continental Army. In 1776, as Washington was preparing in Boston to move against New York, the general requested Congress to send him $250,000 in hard coin to pay off the militia whose term of service had expired. Washington's problem was not to raise the money, but to transport it to Boston past hostile Tories. Shipping the specie by boat and evading the British sea patrol was too hazardous. It was at this juncture that John Hancock called upon "three gentlemen of character" - among them, Moses Franks - to cart the money secretly to Washington's headquarters. It took them two weeks to reach Boston, unfortunately too late to meet the needs of the militia, but the cash was used to satisfy the regulars. The total expense incurred in this trek north amounted to $238.

The fact that 100 or more American Jews may have served in the armed forces is of no great historic significance. Their commercial activities were far more important in an agrarian economy where industry and manufacturing were minimal and the coasts were blockaded by the powerful British fleet. The farmers and townspeople had to have yard goods and tea; it was imperative that the soldiers be supplied with uniforms, blankets, and shoes. One way to relieve the shortage was to arm merchant ships and send them out as privateers to prey on enemy commerce. This Jews did, arming small ships heavily and packing them with large, tough crews who scoured the seas for valuable British cargoes.

Many an American who joined or financed a privateer dreamt of striking it rich. Impoverished Mordecai Sheftall decided to try his luck. After his imprisonment and exile from British-occupied Georgia, he determined on a bold stroke to recoup his losses. In one way or another he managed to secure hold of a twenty-ton sloop, the *Hetty*, sold shares in her to secure working capital, loaded her with thirty men including a Negro slave, and armed her with eight guns, tomahawks, blunderbusses, and boarding pikes. Then he set sail on what was to be a most inglorious adventure. The English captured the *Hetty* and scuttled her, but the persistent Sheftall raised and reoutfitted the vessel. He tried his luck once more, but never struck it rich; indeed, it is questionable whether any of the Jewish merchants of that day made any "big money" lying in wait for British merchantmen.

After a fashion, privateering was a form of blockade-running. Many American ships got through the English naval barrier, for the enemy could not guard every cove and inlet of the long coast. Certainly one of the most daring of the blockade-runners was the firm of Isaac Moses & Co. Its three partners Isaac Moses, Samuel Myers, and Moses Myers had an Amsterdam buying office which shipped their goods to Dutch St. Eustatius in the Caribbean. From there the company's ships made the run to an American port, trusting to fate that they could slip past the cordon set up by the English cruisers. Isaac Moses and his associates were great Whigs. Shortly after the War broke out in 1775, when the Americans set out to conquer Canada, the three partners voluntarily offered the Congress $20,000 in hard currency in exchange for Continental paper which - as they might have foreseen - ultimately proved worthless. If it was any consolation, they received the grateful thanks of John Hancock for their generous gift.

Isaac Moses & Comapny operated on a large scale; Jonas Phillips, of Philadelphia, was not so ambitious. One of Phillips' blockade-running letters, written in July, 1776, has been preserved. It was dispatched via St. Eustatius to an Amsterdam kinsman, a prominent Jewish merchant in that city. Enclosed in the letter was a broadside copy of the Declaration of Independence which had just been published by the Americans. Phillips did not expatiate on the revolt, merely remarking laconically that the Americans had 100,000 soldiers, the British 25,000 and a fleet. What was going to happen? Only God knew, but before the war was over England would be bankrupt. In an appendix to the letter, Phillips got down to business, asking for cloth, apparel, notions, and medicines. The letter was written in Yiddish, no doubt with the expectation that if the British intercepted it, they would let it go by because they could not read it. That was a vain hope, for the ship, which sailed from St. Eustatius, was taken, the letter was impounded, and just because the English could not read it, they concluded that it was in code. It rests today in the English Public Records office in Chancery Lane.

Since the quartermaster department of the Revolutionary armed forces was primitive and inadequate, the government turned to civilian purveyors for badly needed supplies. Many, if not most, Jewish merchants of that day were purveyors on a large or small scale, offering the government clothing, gunpowder, and lead. Harassed for lack of funds, the authorities took their time before settling accounts; some trusting suppliers were never paid at all. One of the merchants who were never reimbursed for their advances was Levy Solomons, of Canada, a brother-in-law of the ebullient David Salisbury Franks. Solomons, a Whig, served the American troops in Canada in 1775 and 1776, helping them establish hospitals and lending them money. When the Americans were forced to retreat, this zealous patriot provided the sick and the wounded with transportation on their way to the border. The British, knowing where his loyalties lay, seized his goods and furniture on July 4, 1776, and threw them into the street; his neighbors shunned him and refused him shelter.

The Jewish businessmen of the period were nothing if not ingenious; there was no supply job that they would not undertake. Exiled to Philadelphia, the New York fur trader Hayman Levy became a garment manufacturer producing breeches and shirts in the local poorhouse. The tailor Levy Marks petitioned Congress - unsuccessfully - to give him the job of superintending the manufacture of army uniforms. Levy's cousins, Barnard and Michael Gratz, turned to anything that offered a profit. They exported tobacco from Virginia, outfitted troops, and shipped supplies to George Rogers Clark, who was dedicated to the task of driving the British out of the western frontier. Michael Gratz's father-in-law, Joseph Simon, a Pennsylvania pioneer, manufactured rifles in Lancaster with his gunsmith partner, William Henry. Out on the Ohio frontier, one of Simon's companies, Simon & Campbell, provided the Indian commissioners with goods for pacifying the natives. The Gratzes performed the same service in New York State, where the Iroquois had to be held in check. The Americans could not afford to fight on two fronts: against Indians in the back country as well as the English in the East. In short, the Jewish importers, wholesalers, and blockade-runners managed - no one really knows how - to ferret out goods even in the darkest of days. The shopkeepers distributed them. This relatively successful job of keeping commodities flowing was the real Jewish contribution to the war effort.

SOURCE: Jacob R. Marcus (ed.), *Jews and the American Revolution: A Bicentennial Documentary* (Cincinnati, 1974), pp. 106-112. Reprinted by permission of Jacob R. Marcus.

7. The Death of Francis Salvador - 1776

*This letter recounts the story of Francis Salvador's (1747-1776)
death. An English-born Jew who became an avid patriot after settling in
South Carolina in December 1773, Salvador was the first unconverted
Jew to serve either in a provincial or "American" legislative body. When
the British attacked, in June 1776, Salvador volunteered to serve in the
militia, led by his fellow congressman, Major Andrew Williamson. Falling in battle, he was probably the first Jew to die fighting for the new
American Republic.*

Camp, two miles below Keowee,
August 4th, 1776

Sir:

I received your Excellency's favours of the 26th and 27th ult. by
express. . . . In my last letter to your Excellency, of the 31st ult., I
informed you of my spies being returned with two white prisoners; who
gave an account of [Alexander] Cameron's being arrived from over the
Hills with twelve white men; and, that he, with the Seneca and other
Indians, were encamped at Ocnore Creek, about thirty miles distant
from Twenty-Three Mile Creek, where I then lay encamped. This intelligence induced me to march immediately to attack their camp, before
they could receive any information of my being so far advanced.

I accordingly marched about six o'clock in the evening, with three
hundred and thirty men on horseback (taking the two prisoners with
me, to show where the enemy were encamped; and told them before I
set out, if I found they deceived me, I would order them instantly to be
put to death), intending to surround their camp by day-break and to
leave our horses about two miles behind, with a party of men to guard
them. The River Keowee lying in our route, and only passable at a ford
at Seneca, obliged me (though much against my inclination) to take
that road; the enemy either having discovered my march, or laid themselves in ambush with a design to cut off any spies or party I had sent
out, had taken possession of the first houses in Seneca and posted
themselves behind a long fence, on an eminence close to the road where
we were to march. And, to prevent being discovered, had filled up the
openings betwixt the rails with twigs of trees and corn-blades. They
suffered the guides and advanced guard to pass when a gun from the
house was discharged meant, as I suppose, for a signal for those placed
behind the fence, who, a few seconds after, poured in a heavy fire upon
my men, which being unexpected, staggered my advanced party.

Here, Mr. Salvador received three wounds and fell by my side. . . .
My horse was shot down under me, but I received no hurt. Lieutenant
Farar of Captain Prince's company immediately supplied me with his.
I desired him to take care of Mr. Salvador, but before he could find him

in the dark the enemy unfortunately got his scalp, which was the only one taken. Captain Smith, son of the late Captain Aaron Smith, saw the Indian, but thought it was his servant taking care of his master or could have prevented it. He died, about half after two o'clock in the morning, forty-five minutes after he received the wounds, sensible to the last. When I came up to him, after dislodging the enemy and speaking to him, he asked, whether I had beat the enemy. I told him yes. He said he was glad of it and shook me by the hand - and bade me farewell - and said he would die in a few minutes. Two men died in the morning; and six more who were badly wounded I have since sent down to the settlements and given directions to Doctors Delahowe and Russell to attend them.

I remained on the ground till day-break and burnt the houses on this side of the river; and afterwards crossed the river the same day - reduced Seneca entirely to ashes. Knowing that the Indians would carry immediate intelligence of my strength to the place where Cameron lay encamped, who would directly move from thence; and having ordered the detachment from Colonels Neel's and Thomas' regiments to attack and destroy Estatoe, Qualhatchie, and Toxaway, and join me this day at Sugar Town, obliged me to march that way, which this day a strong detachment consisting of four hundred men has totally reduced to ashes. An old Indian was found there, who said the enemy had deserted the town four days ago on hearing by a white man that an army was advancing against them.

I am respectfully,
Your Excellency's most obt. servt.
A. Williamson

His Excellency John Rutledge,
President of So. Carolina, Charlestown.

8. The Wounding of Solomon Bush - 1777

One of the first Jews to be wounded in the Revolutionary struggle, Solomon Bush (1753-1795), describes in this letter his wartime activities. Bush, son of a prominent Jewish merchant, distinguished himself in the battle to save Philadelphia, and even after his capture, in 1777, managed to convey important intelligence to George Washington. In 1779, following his parole by the British, he was made a lieutenant-colonel, the highest rank attained by a Jew in a combat unit of the Continental Army. This letter is addressed to Henry Lazarus, a merchant in Frederick Towne, Maryland.

Chestnut Hill
15th Nov' 1777

Dr Sir:

As Mr. Simons letter tells me that he is going to your Town cannot omit leting my good Friend give him satisfaction to hear from his friends. I suppose you heard of my being wounded the 18th of Sept' when with dificulty was bro' home in a most deplorable condition with my thigh broke and the surgeons pronounced my wound Mortal 7 days after the Enemy came: who treated our family with the utmost respect: they did not take the least trifle from us, though our neighbours, the poor Tories lost every thing, Howe's March this way has made many wigs - I was Concealed after the British Army came here 22 Days and shou'd have got Clear but a Vilain gave information of me when I was waited on by an officer what took my Parole when I wrote a line to the Commanding Officer leting him know of my being a prisoner and requesting a Surgeon which he imedeately Comply'd with and was attended every Day during their stay at this place; I am thank God geting better and have the Satisfaction to have my Limb perfectly Strait, my wishes are to be able to get Satisfaction and revenge the Rongs of my injured Country, I wish you joy of our Troops to the Northward and hope to tell you New York is ours before long, the shiping is not got up to Philadelphia though this is the 9th time of their attacking the Fort; there is a Cannonade whilst I am writing shou'd they not be able to Carry the Fort their stay in Philad^a will be short; as it grows late and am seting in bed writing

Remain with my best Wishes to Mr. Mrs. Lazarus uncle Levy and the worthy Miss Brandla

Your most affectionate
Friend & Hbl Servt
Sol^m Bush

9. The Capture of Mordecai Sheftall - 1778

In this retrospective account, Mordecai Sheftall (see Document 1), one of Georgia's earliest and staunchest Whig leaders and a very prominent businessman in Savannah, records the story of his capture by the British. Sheftall was appointed in 1777 to the general staff of the Georgia Brigade with the titular rank of Colonel, and rose to become Commissary General of Purchases and Issues. In 1778, he was appointed Deputy Commissary General of Issues to the Continental Troops in South Carolina and Georgia by General Robert Howe. Before his appointment could be confirmed by Congress, however, the city of Savannah fell to the British and Sheftall was taken captive.

This day [December 29, 1778] the British troops, consisting of about 3,500 men, including two battalions of Hessians under the command of Lieutenant Colonel Archibald Campbell of the Seventy-first Regiment of Highlanders, landed early in the morning at Brewton Hill, two miles below the town of Savannah, where they met with very little opposition before they gained the height. At about three o'clock p.m. they entered and took possession of the town of Savannah, when I endeavored, with my son Sheftall, to make our escape across Musgrove Creek, having first premised that an intrenchment had been thrown up there in order to cover a retreat, and upon seeing Colonel Samuel Elbert and Major John Habersham endeavour to make their escape that way.

But on our arrival at the creek, after having sustained a very heavy fire of musketry from the light infantry under the command of Sir James Baird, during the time we were crossing the Common, without any injury to either of us, we found it high water. And my son not knowing how to swim, and we with about 186 officers and privates being caught, as it were, in a pen, and the Highlanders keeping up a constant fire on us, it was thought advisable to surrender ourselves prisoners, which we accordingly did. And which was no sooner done than the Highlanders plundered every one amongst us, except Major Low, myself, and son, who, being foremost, had an opportunity to surrender ourselves to the British officer, namely, Lieutenant Peter Campbell, who disarmed us as we came into the yard formerly occupied by Mr. Moses Nunes.

During this business Sir James Baird was missing, but on his coming into the yard, he mounted himself on the stepladder which was erected at the end of the house and sounded his brass bugle horn, which the Highlanders no sooner heard than they all got about him, when he addressed himself to them in Highland language, when they all dispersed and finished plundering such of the officers and men as had been fortunate enough to escape their first search. This over, we were marched in file, guarded by the Highlanders and [New] York Volunteers who had come up before we were marched, when we were paraded before Mrs. Goffe's door on the Bay, where we saw the greatest part of the army drawn up.

From there, after some time, we were all marched through the town to the courthouse, which was very much crowded, the greatest part of the officers they had taken being here collected and indiscriminately put together. I had been here about two hours, when an officer, who I afterwards learned to be Major Crystie, called for me by name and ordered me to follow him, which I did, with my blanket and shirt under my arm, my clothing and my son's, which were in my saddlebags, having been taken from my horse, so that my wardrobe consisted of what I had on my back.

On our way to the white guardhouse we met with Colonel Campbell, who inquired of the major who he had got there. On his naming me to him, he desired that I might be well-guarded, as I was a very great rebel. The major obeyed his orders, for, on lodging me in the guardhouse, he ordered the sentry to guard me with a drawn bayonet and not to suffer me to go without the reach of it, which orders were strictly complied with until a Mr. Gild Busler, their commissary general, called for me and ordered me to go with him to my stores, that he might get some provisions for our people, who, he said, were starving, not having eaten anything for three days, which I contradicted, as I had victualled them that morning for the day.

On our way to the office where I used to issue the provisions, he ordered me to give him information of what stores I had in town and what I had sent out of town, and where. This I declined doing, which made him angry. He asked me if I knew that Charlestown [South Carolina] was taken. I told him: "No." He then called us poor, deluded wretches, and said, "Good God! how are you deluded by your leaders!" When I inquired of him who had taken it, and when, he said, General [James] Grant, with 10,000 men, and that it had been taken eight or ten days ago, I smiled and told him it was not so, as I had a letter in my pocket that was wrote in Charlestown but three days ago by my brother.

He replied we had been misinformed. I then retorted that I found they could be misinformed by their leaders, as well as we could be deluded by ours. This made him so angry that when he returned me to the guardhouse, he ordered me to be confined amongst the drunken solders and negroes, where I suffered a great deal of abuse and was threatened to be run through the body or, as they termed it, "skivered" by one of the York Volunteers, which threat he attempted to put into execution three times during the night, but was prevented by one Sergeant Campbell.

In this situation I remained two days without a morsel to eat, when a Hessian officer named Zaltman, finding I could talk his language, removed me to his room and sympathized with me on my situation. He permitted me to send to Mrs. [Abigail] Minis, who sent me some victuals. He also permitted me to go and see my son, and to let him come and stay with me. He introduced me to Captain Kappel, also a Hessian, who treated me very politely.

In this situation I remained until Saturday morning, the second of January, 1779, when the commander, Colonel Innis, sent his orderly for me and [my] son to [go to] his quarters, which was John Habersham's house, where on the top of the step I met with Captain Stanhope, of the "Raven," sloop of war, who treated me with the most illiberal abuse and, after charging me with having refused the supplying of the King's ships with provisions, and of having shut the church door, together with many ill-natured things, ordered me on board the prison ship, together with my son. I made a point of giving Mr. Stanhope suitable answers to his impertinent treatment and then turned from him and inquired for Colonel Innis. I got his leave to go to Mrs. Minis for a shirt she had taken to wash for me, as it was the only one I had left except the one on my back, and that was given me by Captain Kappel, as the British soldiers had plundered both mine and my son's clothes.

This favour he granted me under guard, after which I was conducted on board one of the flatboats and put on board the prison ship "Nancy," commanded by Captain Samuel Tait, when the first thing that presented itself to my view was one of our poor Continental soldiers laying on the ship's main deck in the agonies of death, and who expired in a few hours. After being presented to the captain with mine and the rest of the prisoners' names, I gave him in charge what paper money I had, and my watch. My son also gave him his money to take care of. He appeared to be a little civiller after this confidence placed in him, and permitted us to sleep in a stateroom, that is, the Rev. Moses Allen, myself, and son. In the evening we were served with what was called our allowance, which consisted of two pints and a half [of water?], and a half gill of rice, and about seven ounces of boiled beef per man. We were permitted to choose our messmates, and I accordingly made choice of Capt. Thomas Fineley, Rev. Mr. Allen, Mr. Moses Valentonge, Mr. Daniel Flaherty, myself, and son Sheftall Sheftall.

10. A Disloyalty Charge Refuted - 1778

*A charge of disloyalty was levelled against Savannah Jews, and pub-
lished in* The Charlestown Gazette *December 1, 1778. This pseu-
donymous letter is a reply, published in* The South-Carolina and American General Gazette *on December 3 and addressed John Wells, the
paper's publisher. As we know from other sources, when the British
invaded, in November 1778, Mordecai Sheftall and a number of other
Savannah Jews did, in fact, send their families to Charleston. But they
themselves remained to fight the enemy advancing from Florida and New
York, and Sheftall was captured (Document 9).*

Mr. Wells:

On perusing Mrs. Crouch and Co's paper of the 1st instant
[December 1, 1778], I was extremely surprised to find, in a piece signed
An American, a signature sufficient to lead every honest and judicious
man to imagine that whatever was said in so publick a manner should
be ingenuous and true, assertions directly contrary. Here are his words:

"Yesterday being by my business posted in a much frequented
corner of this town, I observed, in a small space of time, a number of
chairs [chaises] and loaded horses belonging to those who journeyed,
come into town. Upon inspection of their faces and enquiry, I found
them to be of the *Tribe of Israel* who, after taking every advantage in
trade the times admitted of in the State of Georgia, as soon as it was
attacked by an enemy, fled here for an asylum with their ill-got wealth,
dastardly turning their backs upon the country, when in danger, which
gave them bread and protection. Thus it will be in this State if it
should ever be assailed by our enemies. Let judgment take place."

I am apt to think, Mr. Printer, that the gentleman is either very
blind, or he is willing to make himself so. For I am well convinced had
he taken the trouble of going closer to the chairs he would have found
that what he has thus publickly asserted was erroneous, and a palpable
mistake, as he might have been convinced they were of the female
kind, with their dear babes, who had happily arrived at an asylum
where a tyrannical enemy was not at theirs or their dear offsprings'
heels.

I do, therefore, in vindication of many a worthy Israelite now in
Georgia, assert that there is not at this present hour a single Georgia
Israelite in Charles Town. And that so far to the contrary of that
gentleman's assertion, I do declare to the public that many merchants
of that State were here on the 22nd ult. [November], and on being
informed of the enemy landing, they instantly left this [town], as many
a worthy Gentile knows, and proceeded post haste to Georgia, leaving
all their concerns unsettled, and are now with their brother citizens in

the field, doing that which every honest American should do.

The truth of this assertion will in the course of a few days be known to gentlemen of veracity who are entitled to the appellation of Americans. The Charlestown Israelites, I bless Heaven, hitherto have behaved as staunch as any other citizens of this state, and I hope their further conduct will be such as will invalidate the malicious and designing fallacy of the author of the piece alluded to.

I am, sir, yours, etc.,
A real *American*
and
True hearted *Israelite*

Charlestown, Wednesday, December 2, 1778.

11. Refugees in Leicester - 1779

Aaron Lopez portrays here the human difficulties facing individuals forced to flee their city in the wake of the enemy's advance. Lopez (1731-1782), the outstanding Jewish merchant and colonial trader of Newport (see Chapter Two), reported in this letter to Joseph Anthony of Philadelphia (Feburary 3, 1779) on the safe evacuation of his family to Leicester, Massachusetts.

My Dear and very worthy Friend,

How shall I express my gratitude to you for the satisfaction you have given me with the rec't of your friendly and obliging Favor of the 27th ulto. which this moment has been handed me by our mutual Friend Mr. Hewes, who telling me its Bearer returns again to Exeter tomorrow morning, I would not miss the opportunity of acknowledging its agreeable contents, and gratifying your wishes of hearing from me, from my family, and some thing from the distress'd Inhabitants of our once flourishing I[s]land; But before I render you this intelligence, permit me to tell you, that I am extreamly happy to learn, that the Almighty has been pleased to guide you and good Family to so safe an Asylum, and that *there* he has blest you with health, peace, and plenty arround you, during these times of publick and almost universal Calamity; But what I esteem still a greater Blessing, endowed you with a gratefull heart, susceptible of all those divine bounties, which I pray may be continued you with all the additional felicities this sublunary World is capable of affording. For my part I have the pleasure to acquaint my good Friend, that I consider myself under still greater obligations to Heaven; having hitherto enjoy'd every one of those inestimable Blessings you are pleased to tell me of, without the least Merit or Title to them; am therefore to acknowledge myself infinitely more thankfull for so mercifull Dispensations.

Since we left our Island my principal object was to look out for a Spot, where I could place my Family, secured from sudden Allarms and the Cruel Ravages of an enraged Enemy; Such a one I have hitherto found in the small inland Township of Leicester in the Massachusetts Bay, *where* I pitch'd my Tent, erecting a proportionable one to the extent of my numerous Family on the Sumit of an high healthy Hill, where we have experienc'd the civilities and hospitality of a kind Neighbourhood; and moved in the same Sphere of Business I have been used to follow, which, altho much more contracted, it has fully answer'd my wishes, and you know my Friend, when that is the case, it never fails of constituting real happiness: Add to this the satisfaction of having for a next door neighbour your truly well wishing Friend, my Father in Law Mr. Rivera, who with his Family I left in good health, spending in peace the fruits of his last summer's Labour on a small Farm, the Old Gentleman improves with much the same *Farming Faculties*, you tell me you cultivate yours; and I can further inform you that while his hands have been imploy'd in that usefull Art, his agitated Mind has uniformly accompanied yours to poor Newport; where I do still hope we shall soon have the pleasure of meeting each other again and re-enjoy those injurd habitations, we have so long been deprived of, with all satisfaction.

By this Weeks Post Mrs. Lopez has informed me that the Widow Lee, who had the Liberty of going down from Providence in a Flag to Newport, after staying there some days, she had the indulgency of returning to Providence, and being engaged to nurse my Daughter Mrs. Mendez (who I have the consolation to tell you leaves [lives] also near me and next door to our good Neighbour Capt. Jno. Lyon formerly of Newport). This Mrs. Lee coming directly on her return into our Family inform'd Mrs. Lopez, that the poor Inhabitants of that Town, have been very much distress'd this Winter for the want of fewell and provisions, those Individuals of my Society in particular, who she said had not tasted any meat, but once in two months: Fish there was none at this Season of the Year, and they were reduced to the alternative of leaving upon Chocolate and Coffe. These and many other Callamities and Insults the wretched Inhabitants experience, ought to excite our thanks to that Great Being, who gave us resolution to exchange at so early a period that melancholy Spot for that we now are enjoying. Your Dweling house I understand has sufer'd much. Your Neighbour Augustus Johnson was found dead at his house. My Neighbour Gideon Sesson's Wife is crazy, and what I lament most, is, that the vertue of several of our Reputable Ladys has been attacked and sullied by our destructive Enemys, - so much for poor Newport. Capt. Benj. Wright continues at Jamaica, his zeallous wishes to put me in possession of some part of the large property I have had lock'd up in his hands since the commencement of this war, led him to address me with three Vessels loaded on my sole and proper account, all which have been taken by our American Cruizers; the first falling in honest hands was delivered up to me by a reference agreed to by the parties. The other two were libelled and contested, one of them was adjudged at Providence to be restored to me: the opposite party appealed to Congress. The third and most valuable was (contrary to the opinion and expectation of every spectator) condemn'd at a Connecticut Court of Admiralty. I appealed to Congress, which has brought me here in full hopes of obtaining redress. Mrs. Wright was left poorly at Newport, when Nurse Lee came away, which prevented Mrs. Wright coming off in the same Flagg, as she intended, but will do it soon, as she recovers.

I have oferd the poor distress'd Woman all the assistance in my power to grant her, as I esteeme her an object of real merit.

Now my Dear Friend I have only to add my sincere thanks for your kind invitation to spend a day or two with you at your habitation. I shall inform myself (not being acquainted where Exeter lays) and if I can always make it convenient to call on you, may expect to see me; meantime permit me to announce you and Mrs. Anthony every good wish pure esteem can suggest being very truly, Dear Sir, Your affectionate Friend and humble Servant.

12. Isaac Moses Petitions the Continental Congress - 1779

*In this petition, dated July 27, 1779, Isaac Moses (1742-1818)
requests the Continental Congress to supply gunpowder for his privateers.
Moses, one of the wealthiest and most prominent merchant-shippers of
his day, left New York when the British occupied it and reestablished
himself in Philadelphia. By having his ships run the British blockade, he
helped provide the Continental Congress with strategic goods while simultaneously reaping the financial rewards of this risky but profitable
endeavor.*

To the Honorable the Congress of the United States of North
America:

The petition of Isaac Moses, now of the city of Philadelphia, merchant, most humbly sheweth:

That your petitioner, having loaded a schooner, letter of marque,
and fitted her with every necessary but gun powder, in a warlike
manner, has made all the search in his power for that article, but
finding himself every where dissappointed, is now under the dissagree-
able necessity of troubling Your Honours, and to pray that you would
be pleased to spare him, out of the public stores, two or three hundred
weight of powder.

He flatters himself his principals as a true Whig and friend to the
liberties of this country are so well known to some of your members,
that it is needless to mention them here, or to remind your body of the
assistance he has afforded these United States from time to time in the
importation of divers articles which he spared them, but particularly
when he and his partners spared these states upwards of twenty
thousand dollars in specie, in exchange for Continental dollars, at the
time the Canada expedition was on foot, and for which they received
the thanks from or through your then president, the Honourable John
Hancock, Esq.

Your petitioner submits to your honourable House to consider how
unsafe it would be in him to risk his property at these times on the
high seas without having proper means of defence with it, and pledges
himself either immediately to pay for the powder, or to reemburse the
public with an equal quantity of that article, and that either on the
return of his vessel, or at the time that she ought to return.

Your petitioner therefore flatters himself your honourable House
will be pleased on these considerations to grant him his request;

And he, as in duty bound, will every pray.

Isaac Moses

13. Mordecai Sheftall Pleads for Relief - 1780

This petition is sadly typical of those sent by Jews (and non-Jews) requesting compensation for monies advanced to the patriots' cause or for losses sustained in the fighting. War and imprisonment had depleted the fortune of Mordecai Sheftall (Documents 1, 9) and cost him all his property; he was reduced to pleading. While Congress did ultimately settle with him, he received only about 5% of what he claimed to be owed. Like many people involved in financing or supplying the Continental forces, he ended up losing a fortune.

To his Excellency, the President and the
Honorable Members of Congress:

The memorial of Mordecai Sheftall humbly sheweth that your memorialist was appointed Deputy Commissary General of Issues in the State of Georgia,

That his attention to the wants of the army in that quarter led him to make advances for their support at those times when no Continental money was sent by Congress for the support of the troops there,

That your memorialist had also a considerable sum due to him which in the present state of depreciation would amount on receiving the same to a literal nonpayment,

That a long and painful captivity has reduced your memorialist to very distressed circumstances which are still heighten'd by having a wife and foure children in Charles Town deprived of every means of subsisting.

Your memorialist humbly subjoynes an acco't and submits his situation to Congress, requesting they will pleas to take his case into consideration and afforde him such relief, in the whole or in part, as the wisdom and humanity of the Honorable Congress will thinke expedient, to assist him in removing his family from the miseries the[y] now labour under.

And your memorialist will every pray.

                                    Mordecai Sheftall

Philadelphia,
Aug't 21, 1780.

14. Loyalist Rachel Myers Pleads for Relief - 1780

Jewish loyalists suffered privation too. When Newport was recaptured from the British in 1780, the widow Rachel Myers and her large family moved to New York City which continued under Loyalist occupation. Being without any means of support, she wrote to Sir Henry Clinton, commander in chief of all British forces in North America, describing her plight and requesting assistance.

To His Excellency, Sir Henry Clinton, Knight of the Most Honorable Order of the Bath, General and Commander in Chief, etc., etc., etc.

The petition of Rachel Myers, late of Newport, widow, humbly sheweth:

That your petitioner was for many years an inhabitant of Newport, where she supported, by her industry, a large family of children;

That from the decissive part her son, Benjamin Myers, took with the associated refugees and other loyalists at Rhode Island, she was obliged to leave that place after it was evacuated by his Majesty's troops and come to this city in a flag of truce [ship] with all her family, consisting of nine children;

That she has in the maintenance of her family struggled with many difficulties, and from the assistance she has derived from a few benevolent friends, hitherto been able to support, tho indifferently, her children. But all her industry is not now sufficient to afford them the necessaries of life, which constrains her to implore your Excellency to extend her some relief from government, by permitting her to receive for her family such rations of provisions, etc., as may be thought necessary.

And your petitioner, as in duty bound, shall ever pray.

Rachel Myers

New York, April 3, 1781.

15. Robert Morris Sends for Haym Salomon - 1781

Haym Salomon (1740-1785), a native of Poland, arrived in America in 1772 and soon embraced the cause of independence. He helped American prisoners of war escape, was arrested by the British on charges of espionage, escaped to Philadelphia, and quickly became one of the outstanding financial brokers in the new nation. His brokerage office became one of Philadelphia's financial centers. When the French minister to Congress needed a paymaster-general for the French forces in America, he picked Salomon. Robert Morris, following his appointment by Congress in 1781 as Superintendent of Finance, also relied heavily on Salomon, for Salomon sold Morris's bills of exchange, providing funds at low commission rates which helped keep the government solvent. This excerpt from Robert Morris's diary (August 27, 1781) illustrates the kinds of commercial transactions which Salomon undertook. Manuel Josephson (1729-1796) and Isaac Moses (1742-1818), both Jews, also sold bills of exchange on behalf of the Superintendent and competed with Salomon in the brokerage trade.

Sent for Mr Haym Solomon the Jew Broker, who informed me that he had sold small sums of the Pennsylvania State paper at two Dollars for 1 of silver and that he Offered to purchase said paper at 2 ½ for One agreable to Orders I had before given him, and I think it best to continue my Orders on this footing untill the Collection of Taxes Commences. He informed me that bills of Exchange continued to pour in our Market from the Eastern states and other places where the French Bills had been sold or paid and that the best bills of 30 days Sight on France are now selling at 4/6 to 4/9 per five Livres. Mr Josephson says the same and Mr Isaac Moses who offers to purchase bills from me says he can purchase with Cash in hand for 4/6. Mr Moses having an Order on me by Colo. Miles for Amount of Oznaburgs bought sometime, to make sand bags for the intended siege of N York, he requires payment or Offers to take bills for Lrs. 30,000 to Discount this balance and pay the remainder in six Weeks; after much altercation agreed with him at 5/6 to stay Six Week.

16. *"Broker to the Office of Finance" - 1782*

Haym Salomon (Document 15) was granted permission by Robert Morris to advertise himself as Broker to the Office of Finance. As this example from the Freeman's Journal *(November 16, 1782) shows, he took full advantage of this title to boost his prestige and gain a competitive edge against rival brokers.*

Haym Salomons, Broker to the Office of Finance, to the Consul General of France, and to the Treasurer of the French Army, At his office in Front Street, between Market and Arch streets. BUYS and sells on commission BANK STOCK, BILLS of EXCHANGE on France, Spain, Holland, and other parts of Europe, the West-Indies, and inland bills, at the usual commissions.

He buys and sells LOAN OFFICE CERTIFICATES, CONTINEN-TAL and STATE MONEY, of this or any other state, paymaster and quarter-master generals notes; these, and every other kind of paper transactions (bills of exchange excepted) he will charge his employers no more than ONE HALF PER CENT, for his commission.

He procures MONEY on LOAN for a short time and gets notes and bills discounted.

Gentlemen and others, residing in this state, or any of the United States, by sending their orders to the office, may depend on having their business transacted with as much fidelity and expedition as if they were themselves present.

He receives tobacco, sugars, tea, and every other sort of goods, to sell on commission, for which purpose he has provided proper stores.

He flatters himself his assiduity, punctuality, and extensive connections in his business, as a broker, is well established in various parts of Europe, and in the United States in particular.

All persons who shall please to favour him with their business may depend upon his utmost exertion for their interest, and PART of the MONEY ADVANCED, if desired.

CHAPTER IV

A COMMUNITY TRANSFORMED

The American Revolution transformed American Jewish life. New Jewish communities emerged, others went into eclipse. Peace opened up new economic opportunities, which Jews were able to avail themselves of. The free, democratic spirit of the age permeated even into the synagogue, resulting in new synagogue constitutions and, in one case, in a Jewish "bill of rights." Taking pride in the part they played in the battle for independence, and much like their non-Jewish neighbors, Jews reveled in the freedom which the new nation promised (see Chapter V, "The New Nation and the Jews"). While heady predictions of a *novus ordo seclorum* (new order of the ages) proved premature, the Revolution did alter the character of the American Jewish community. At the same time, it brought Jews and their neighbors into closer contact and harmony with one another.

THE IMPACT OF THE AMERICAN REVOLUTION ON AMERICAN JEW̌

Jonathan D. Sarna

Jonathan Sarna's analysis of the Revolution's impact shows how the war and its aftermath affected Jewish life not only in the eighteenth century, but ever afterwards as well. Sarna is particularly interested in the relationship of Jews and non-Jews in America. In this selection, he shows how on a variety of levels the Revolution altered this relationship, influencing even the inner life of the synagogue.

Wartime migrations had lasting effects. People who never had met Jews discovered them for the first time, and learned how similar they were to everyone else. Jews from different parts of the country encountered one another, and cemented lasting unions. A succession of Jewish marriages took place, as Jewish children made new friends. Finally, the distribution of Jews in the colonies changed. Newport, Rhode Island, formerly one of the four largest Jewish communities in America had its port destroyed in the war. Its Jews scattered. The Savannah Jewish community also suffered greatly from the war's decimating effects. On the other hand, two cities that were spared destruction, Philadelphia and Charleston, emerged from the war with larger and better organized Jewish communities than they had ever known before.

In addition to geographical mobility, the Revolution fostered economic mobility among American Jews. Trade disruptions and wartime hazards took their toll, especially on traditional, old stock Jewish merchants like the Gomezes and Frankses. Their fortunes declined enormously. On the other hand, adventurous entrepreneurs - young, fearless and innovative upstarts - emerged from the war wealthy men. Haym Salomon bounded up the economic ladder by making the best both of his formidable linguistic talents, and of his newly learned advertising and marketing techniques. He and his heirs seem not to have adapted as well to the inflationary postwar economy, for when he died his family became impoverished. Uriah Hendricks, and Hessian immigrants like Alexander Zuntz, Jacob and Philip Marc, and Joseph Darmstadt rose to the top more slowly. But by the early nineteenth century all were established and prospering. Generally speaking, the postwar decades were years of progress in the United States. Opportunities were available, and Jews, like their non-Jewish neighbors, made the most of them.

In order to take advantage of postwar economic opportunities, Jews sometimes compromised their ritual observances. They violated the Sabbath; they ate forbidden foods; and they ignored laws regarding family purity. War conditions had encouraged such laxities: the few Jews who struggled to observe the commandments while under arms are remembered precisely because they were so unique. Postwar America also encouraged such laxities. While religious denominations scrambled to adapt to independence, many parishioners abandoned their churches for other activities. "Pious men complained that the war had been a great demoralizer. Instead of awakening the community to a lively sense of the goodness of God, the license of war made men weary of religious restraint," John B. McMaster observed. He likely exaggerated. Historians no longer believe that the postwar religious depression was quite so severe. Still, McMaster's comment demonstrates that Jews did not simply leave Shearith Israel empty on Saturday morning for business reasons. They also were caught up in the lackadaisical religious spirit of the age.

Formerly, American Jews had imitated the example of the Anglican Church, the church that was officially established in many of the colonies. Synagogues modelled themselves on the Bevis Marks Synagogue in England, and looked to the Mother Country for guidance and assistance. After the Revolution, congregations prudently changed their constitutions (actually, they wrote "constitutions" for the first time; before 1776 they called the laws they were governed by "Hascamoth"). They became more independent, and discarded as unfashionable leadership forms that looked undemocratic. At Shearith Israel, in 1790, the franchise was widened (though not as far as it would be in other synagogues), a new constitution was promulgated, and a "bill of rights" was drawn up. The new set of laws began with a ringing affirmation of popular sovereignty reminiscent of the American Constitution: "We the members of K.K. Shearith Israel." Another paragraph explicitly linked Shearith Israel with the "state happily constituted upon the principles of equal liberty, civil and religious." Still a third paragraph, the introduction to the new "bill of rights" (which may have been written at a different time) justified synagogue laws in terms that Americans would immediately have understood:

> Whereas in free states all power originates and is derived from the people, who always retain every right necessary for their well being individually, and, for the better ascertaining those rights with more precision and explicitly, from [form?] a declaration or bill of those rights. In a like manner the individuals of every society in such state are entitled to and retain their several rights, which ought to be preserved inviolate.

> Therefore we, the profession [professors] of the Divine Laws, members of this holy congregation of Shearith Israel, in the city of New York, conceive it our duty to make this declaration of our rights and privileges.

Congregation Beth Shalome of Richmond followed this same rhetorical practice. It began its 1789 constitution with the words "We the subscribers of the Israelite religion resident in this place desirous of promoting divine worship," and continued in awkward, seemingly immigrant English to justify synagogue laws in American terms:

> It is necessary that in all societies that certain rules and regulations be made for the government for the same as tend well to the proper decorum in a place dedicated to the worship of the Almighty God, peace and friendship among the same.

It then offered membership and voting privileges to "every free man residing in this city for the term of three months of the age of 21 years . . . who congregates with us."

By inviting, rather than obligating all Jews to become members, Beth Shalome signalled its acceptance of the "voluntary principle" in religion. Like Protestant churches it began to depend on persuasion rather than coercion. This change did not come about without resistance. In 1805, Shearith Israel actually attempted to collect a tax of ten dollars from all New York Jews "that do not commune with us." But the trend was clear. The next few decades would see the slow transition from a coercive "synagogue-community" to a more voluntaristic "community of synagogues." As early as 1795, Philadelphia became the first city in America with two different synagogues. By 1830, the number of synagogues in New York alone numbered fifteen.

The voluntary principle and synagogue democracy naturally resulted in synagogues that paid greater heed to members' needs and desires. Congregational officers knew that dissatisfied Jews could abandon a synagogue or weaken it through competition. In response to congregant demands, some synagogues thus began to perform conversions, something they had previously hesitated to do for historical and halachic reasons. Other synagogues showed new leniency toward Jews who intermarried or violated the Sabbath. Leaders took their cue from congregants: they worried less about Jewish law, and more about "being ashamed for the Goyim . . . hav[ing] a stigma cast upon us and be[ing] derided."

The twin desires of post-Revolutionary American Jews - to conform and to gain acceptance - made decorum and Americanization central synagogue concerns. In the ensuing decades, mainstream Protestant customs, defined by Jews as respectable, exercised an ever greater influence on American Jewish congregational life. Not all changes, of course, reflect conscious imitation. When Christian dates replaced Jewish dates in some congregational minutes, for example, the shift probably reveals nothing more than the appointment of a new secretary - a more Americanized one. When Jewish leaders consulted "with different members of Religious Incorporated Societies in this city," and followed their standards, they also in all likelihood acted innocently, without giving a thought to how far social intercourse had evolved from the days when Jews only observed non-Jews in order to learn what *not* to do. Some, however, were fully conscious that Jews' accepted point of reference had become respectable Protestantism, and they turned this knowledge to their own advantage. When Gershom Seixas haggled with congregational officers about a raise, for example, he offered to submit his dispute to "three or five citizens of any religious society" for arbitration. He knew that an appeal to Christian practice was the easiest way to obtain redress from his fellow Jews.

SOURCE: Jonathan D. Sarna, "The Impact of the American Revolution on American Jews," *Modern Judaism* 1 (1981), pp. 151-152, 155-157. Reprinted by permission of *Modern Judaism*.

17. "We Have the World to Begin Againe" - 1783

This letter shows the great excitement experienced by Georgia patriot Mordecai Sheftall - now far better off financially than in 1780 (Chapter III, Document 13) - at news that the war had ceased and independence been won. Writing to his son, Sheftall Sheftall, Mordecai Sheftall described his feelings of relief and hope - "we have the world to begin againe." At the same time, Sheftall began figuring the economic consequences of peace, and made plans accordingly.

Savannah, 13 April, 1783.

My dear Son:

Allthoe I wrote you on Friday last, yet so happy an event haveing taken place, [the declaration of suspension of hostilities between Great Britain and the United States,] as the inclosed will communicate, since my writing, I could not help giving it to you and all my friends by the first and earliest opp[ortunit]'y.

What my feelings are on the occassion is easier immagined than described. For it must be supposed that every real well wisher to his country must feel him self happy to have lived to see this longe and bloody contest brot to so happy an issue. More especially, as we have obetained our independence, instead of those threats of bringing us with submission to the foot of that throne whose greatest mercies to Americans has been nothing but one continued scene of cruelty, of which you as well as my self have experienced our shares.

But, thanks to the Almighty, it is now at an end. Of which happy event I sincerly congratulate you and all my freinds. As an intier new scene will open it self, and we have the world to begin againe, I would have you come home as soon after the [Passover] hollidays as possibly you can. As I shall plan a voyage for you to execute which will requier dispatch.

If you have not purchased the linen directed, don't buy more than one piece, as goods must be very low in a very short time. Let Mr. Jacobs have this news as soon as possible, as the knowledge of it for a few hours, before 'tis published, may be of the outmost consiquence to a man in trade. And I really wish I could be a means of his and Mr. Cohen, in particular, benefitting by a knowledge of it in time.

Your mother, brothers, and sisters are all well and give theire love to you and compliments to all freinds. I am

Your affectionate father,
Mordecai Sheftall

[P.S.] Give my love to your Uncle Levi and family. Hetty says she fears that you have spent her money instead of buying her scisars, as there are none come to hand for her. For fear that I forgot to mention the arrival of the things you sent by George, I now inform you that they are.

18. *Gershom Seixas Returns to New York - 1784*

War's end changed the life of the leading American religious figure of the day, Rev. Gershom Seixas of Congregation Shearith Israel in New York. Called back to his home congregation after having spent the war years away, first in Connecticut and then in Philadelphia, Seixas first thanked God and then took the occasion to urge "stricter attention" to the "Rules of Decency and Decorum." He wanted Jews to "command respect" from the non-Jews around them.

The manifold Mercies of Almighty Providence exercised towards us during the Course of a perilous & most distressing War - & our being again restor'd to our former Place of Residence in Peace. it becomes a Duty incumbent on us to exert ourselves as a religious Society to acknowledge our Gratitude to him in every possible Manner, to celebrate his Praises & to glorify his holy Name -

As a just Tribute due to Omnipotence, the Parnass requests the Congregation, that the stricter attention may be paid to the Rules of Decency & Decorum which have a natural tendency to excite Devotion especially in Time of divine Service, which he is sorry to observe has been for some time neglected, but is in Hopes to see this holy Congregation placed on such a Footing as to command Respect, instead of Contempt which they incur by some evil Practices that have obtained thro' the Means of a few weak & inconsiderate set of Men such as Leaving the Synagogue in times of Prayer, talking & laughing with & to each other - he therefore strongly recommends a proper & suitable Behaviour to every One who assembles in this Place & most earnestly exhorts them to consider in whose Presence they are & to Whom they address themselves, & know that it is the Supreme King of Kings, who penetrates the most secret recesses of the Heart, & who is ever ready to hear those who call upon Him in Truth.

He more particularly requires of those who are Parents to enjoin their Children not to commit those Misdemeanors which are so highly reprehensible, but to admonish them on everything that tends to Indecency -

He at the same time takes the Liberty to assure you that he does not mean to arrogate to himself any Power which he is not legally entitled to by the Nature of his Office but is solely actuated by Motives of Zeal for our holy & religious Worship - & from an innate Principles of Benevolence to promote the real Welfare of this Congregation which always has been & is now his chief Study -

Sensible of the Fallability of Man he hesitates not to declare that he is ever open to Conviction, & should he at any time in the Course of his Administration give Occasion of Offence to any Individual, he hopes they will not impute it to Design, as it is his most strenuous Desire to give general Satisfaction.

Convinced of the Difficulties attending those who govern he calls on you all to join Heart & Hand to support him in every thing that is justifiable in the Sight of God & Man - to your own Reason he appeals, & to your Decisions he cheerfully submits -

In full Confidence of your Endeavors to comply with his Requisitions - he rests assured we may attain the consequent Blessings of Peace and humbly prays the Almighty God to continue his Goodness to us & to all Israel. Amen.

19. A "Jew-Broker" Replies - 1784

This open letter offers striking testimony to the freedom and security Jews felt in the wake of the Revolution. Following upon an anti-Jewish attack by Miers Fisher, a Quaker lawyer and former Tory exile, a writer who signed himself "A Jewish Broker," likely Haym Salomon, hit back hard. He accused Fisher of being un-American, answered his attacks, and unleashed a barrage of charges of his own against Fisher and his Quaker associates. In America, as we saw even during the Revolution (Chapter III, Document 10), Jews could respond to anti-Semitism without fear.

[March 13, 1784.]

To Miers Fisher, Esquire:

I must address you, in this manner, although you do not deserve it. Unaccustomed as you are to receive any mark of respect from the public, it will be expected that I should make an apology for introducing a character, *fetid* and *infamous*, like yours, to general notice and attention. Your conspicuous *Toryism* and *disaffection* long since buried you in the silent grave of *popular* oblivion and contempt; and your extraordinary conduct and deportment, in several other respects, has brought and reduced you to that dreary dungeon of insignificance, to that gulph of defeated spirits, from which even the powers of *hope* "that comes to all" cannot relieve or better you.

In this most miserable of all situations, principally arising from an obstinate, inflexible perseverance in your political *heresy* and *schism* (so detestable in itself, so ruinous and destructive to our country, and obnoxious to all around us), you are now left quite destitute and forlorn! Unhappy and disappointed man! Once exiled [September, 1777] and excommunicated by the state, *as a sly, insidious enemy;* severed and detached from the generous bosom of *patriotism* and *public virtue; shunned* and deserted by *faithful friends*, in whom you once so safely trusted; since, debarred and prevented from *your practice* by rule of court as an attorney at the bar; *and excluded* from every other essential and dignified privilege of which the *rest of citizens* can boast - with the wretched remains of a *wrecked* reputation - you exhibit so complete a spectacle of distress and wretchedness, as rather excites one's tenderness than vengeance, and would soften and melt down dispositions more relentless and unforgiving than mine!

But whatever claims of mercy you may demand, on these accounts; whatever I should think, were I to judge you as your *personal* enemy in *private* respects; yet the *forward* and unexampled advances and steps you have lately taken in the concert of *public* affairs; the high-cockaded air of *fancied* importance you now assume; the petulant, discontented humor you have manifested for establishing *a new bank; your longings and pantings to approach our *political vineyard*, and blast the fruits of those labors for which you neither *toiled nor spun*; and more particularly, the indecent, unjust, inhumane aspersions, you cast so indiscriminately on the *Jews* of this city at large, in your arguments of Wednesday week, before the honorable legislature of the commonwealth - these circumstances, if my apprehensions are right, preclude you from any lenity or favor, and present you a fair victim and offering to the sacred altar of public justice.

You are not therefore to expect any indulgence, because you merit none. I daresay you experience it not in your own feelings; nor have you any right whatever to hope for the least tenderness from me. You shall not have it; and if you are cut and smarted with the whip and lashes of my reproach and resentments, if I lay my talons and point out the *ingrate*, if my tongue is clamorous of you and *your odious confederates*, and I should pain the tenderest veins of their breasts - remember, you first gave birth to all yourself, that it arose entirely from you; and in tracing of events hereafter to the source you will, perhaps, find to your sorrow and cost that you are only blameable for whatever consequences have or may arise on the occasion.

You not only endeavoured to injure me by your unwarrantable expressions, but every other person of the same *religious* persuasion I hold, and which the laws of the country, and the glorious toleration and *liberty of conscience*, have allowed me to indulge and adopt. The injury is highly crimsoned and aggravated, as there was no proper reason or ground for your invectives. The attack on the *Jews* seemed wanton, and could only have been premeditated by such a base and degenerate mind as yours. It was not owing to the sudden sallies of passion, or to the warmth of a disconcerted and hasty imagination. I cannot, therefore, place it to the account of meer human frailties, in which your *will* and understanding had no concern, and for which I am always disposed to make every compassionate allowance. And though an individual is not obliged to avenge the injuries of particular societies and sectaries [sects] of men, he is nevertheless called upon, by every dear and serious consideration, to speak his mind freely and independently of public transactions and general events, to assert his own share in the public consequence and to act his part fairly on the social theatre.

Permit me, then, with this view of things, to take notice of these terms of reproach and invective which, considering you as a friend to good manners and decorum, you have heaped on our nation [religious group] and profession with so liberal and unsparing a hand. I am a Jew; it is my own nation and profession. I also subscribe myself a broker, and a broker, too, whose opportunities and knowledge, along with other brokers of his intimate acquaintance, in a great course of business, has made him very familiar and privy to every minute design and artifice of your *wiley colleagues* and associates.

I exult and glory in reflecting that we have the honour to reside in a free country where, as a people, we have met with the most generous countenance and protection; and I do not at all despair, notwithstanding former obstacles [the disabilities imposed by the Pennsylvania Constitution of 1776], that we shall still obtain every other privilege that we aspire to enjoy along with our fellow-citizens. It also affords me unspeakable satisfaction, and is indeed one of the most pleasing employments of my thoughtful moments, to contemplate that we have in general been early uniform, decisive Whigs, and were second to none in our patriotism and attachment to our country!

What but Erinnys (the name of the Furies of Hell) itself could have thus tempted you to wander from the common path of things, and go a stray among *thorns and briars*? What were your motives and inducements for introducing the Jews so disrespectfully into your unhallowed and polluted lips? Who are you, or what are you (a meer *tenant at sufferance*, of your liberty), that in a *free* country you dare to trample on any sectary whatever of people? Did you expect to serve yourself, or your friends and confederates [Tories and pacifist Quakers] - these serpents in our bosom, whose poisonous stings have been darted into every *patriot* character among us?

In any other place, in managing another cause, you might have had patience to attend to the consequences of such unpardonable rashness and temerity. But here you thought yourself safe, and at full leave to take the most unlicensed liberties with characters, in regard of whom you can in no respect pretend to vie! You shall yet repent, even *in sackcloth* and *ashes*, for the foul language in which you have expressed yourself. And neither the interposition of some well meant though mistaken Whigs who, I am sorry to think, have joined you, "nor even the sacred shield of cowardice shall protect you," for your transgressions. Who knows but the beams of that very denomination whom you have traduced may, on one day, perhaps not very remote, warm you into the most abject servility, and make you penitentially solemnize what you have done?

An error is easily remedied, and there may be some compensation for actual injuries. But a downright insult can neither be forgiven or forgot, and seldom admits of atonement or reparation. It is our happiness to live in the times of enlightened liberty, when the human mind, liberated from the restraints and fetters of superstition and authority, hath been taught to conceive just sentiments of its own; and when mankind, in matters of *religion*, are quite charitable and benevolent in their opinions of each other.

Individuals may act improperly, and sometimes deserve censure; but is no less unjust than ungenerous to condemn all for the faults of a few, and reflect generally on a whole community for the indiscretion of some particular persons. There is no body of people but have some exceptionable characters with them; and even your own religious sectary [the Quakers], whom you have compelled me to dissect in the course of this address, are not destitute of *very proper subjects* of criticism and animadversion.

Good citizens who nauseate, and the public who contemn, have heard your invectives against the Jews. Unhappily for you, a long series of enormities have proved you more your own enemy than I am. To you, then, my worthy friends and fellow-citizens (characters teeming with strict candor and disinterestedness), do I turn myself with pleasure from that steril field, from that *Grampian* desart, which hath hitherto employed me.

It is your candor I seek; it is your disinterestedness I solicit. The opinions of *Fisher* and his adherents, whether wilful in their malignity, or sincere in their ignorance, are no longer worthy of my notice. His observations are low; his intentions are too discernable. His whole endeavours centre in one point, namely, to create a *new bank*.

To effect this end, he has spared neither pains or labours. He has said every thing that artifice could dictate, or malice invent. He has betrayed himself in a thousand inconsistencies, and adopted absurdities which, supposing him a man of sense and observation, would have disgraced the lips of an idiot.

And for whom is the new bank meant and intended? For the benefit of men like himself, who have been in general averse and opposed to the war and common cause: for the insurgents against our liberty and independence; for *mercenary* and *artful* citizens, where selfish views are totally incompatible with the happiness of the people; for bifronted political *Janus's*, the meer weathercocks of every breeze and gale that blows.

Who traded with the enemy? Who first depreciated the public currency? Who lent our enemies money to carry on the war? Who were spies and pilots to the British? Who prolonged the war? Who was the cause of so many valuable men losing their lives in the field and *prison-ships*? Who did not pay any taxes? Who has now the public securities in hand? Who would not receive our Continental money? Who has purchased *Burgoyne's* convention bills? Who depreciated the French bills? Who depreciated the bills of the *United States* on Paris? Who slandered the institution of the *Bank of North-America*? Who refused taking *banknotes* when they fi[r]st issued? Who discouraged the people from lodging money in the bank? And are these the characters who talk of instituting a bank for *the good of the public*? Are these the people who want a charter from our legislature? Shall such a bastard progeny of freedom, such jests and phantoms of patriotism and the social virtues be indulged in their wishes? For shame! For shame! Surrender the puerile, the fruitless pretensions! Public honor and public gratitude cry aloud against you, and says, or seems to say, as earnest as your endeavors have been, you shall not have your charter.

From such a *medley* and *group* of characters (an impure nest of vipers, the very *bloodhounds* of our lives and liberties) we have every thing to hazard, and nothing to expect. Suspicion shakes her wary head against them, and experience suggests that the sly, insinuating intrigues and combinations of these persons are to be watched and guarded against as much as possible. Though the *proposals* are generous and captivating, their practices, I will venture to affirm, cannot correspond; and however *fascinating* they may be *in appearance*, their designs are *deep* and *wiley*. With the soft and soothing voice of *Jacob* they may exercise the *hand*, the *hairy* hand of *Esau!*

I shall not inquire whether two banks in a commercial country would not clash with each other, and prove exceeding detrimental and injurious to the community. Having only ventured to give an account of the leading characters who compose the new bank, allow me in conclusion to rectify an error of Mr. Fisher's, who publicly declared, "the Jews were the authors of high and unusual interest." No! The Jews can acquit themselves of this artful imputation, and turn your own batteries on yourself. It was neither the *Jews* or *Christians* that founded the practice, but *Quakers* - and *Quakers* worse than *heathens, pagans*, or *idolaters*; men, though not Jews in *faith*, are yet Jews in *traffic*; men abounding with avarice, *who neither fear God, nor regard man.*

Those very persons who are now flattering themselves with the idea of a new bank, first invented the practise of discounting notes at five per cent. I have retained an alphabetical list of names, as well as the other brokers, and can specify persons, if necessary. In the language of Naphtali [Nathan] to David, I have it in my power to point at the very *would-be* directors, and say: "*Thou art the man.*" I can prove that it were these people, unwilling to venture money in trade during the war, who first declined letting out money on the best mortgage and bond security.

Were they now gratified in their expectations, would they not display the same undue spirit and degrade the dignity of a bank with practices unbecoming a common broker? Is it not in their power to finess at the bank, and refuse discounting notes on purpose to gripe [harm] the necessitous part of the people, and extort improper premiums out of doors [secretly]? And have we not reason to expect this would be the case?

A Jew Broker

20. Mikveh Israel Appeals to the Community for Funds - 1788

A different side of the post-war American Jewish situation is revealed here. Peace had brought about a decline in Philadelphia's Jewish population, as many of those had fled to Philadelphia returned home, while others headed west in search of opportunity. The city's newly built synagogue, Mikveh Israel, stood in debt, in danger of being closed. The emergency fund drive of 1788, documented here, temporarily saved the day. In a show of good will, Philadelphia Christians, Benjamin Franklin among them, joined with Jews in coming up with the requisite funds.

To the Humane, Charitable, well-dispos'd People

The Representation and Solicitation of the good People of the Hebrew Society in the City of Philadelphia, commonly call'd Israelites -

Whereas the religious Order of Men in this City, denominated Israelites, were without any Synagogue, or House of Worship untill the Year 1780 when desirous of accommodating themselves, and encouraged thereto by a number of respectable & worthy brethren of the Hebrew Society then in this Place (who generously contributed to the Design) they purchased a Lot of Ground, & erected thereon the Buildings necessary & proper for their religious Worship. And whereas many of their Number at the Close of the late War, return'd to New York, Charleston, & elsewhere their Homes (which they had been exiled from, & obliged to leave on account of their Attachment to American Measures) leaving the remaining few of their Religion here, burthen'd with a considerable Charge consequent from so great an Undertaking. And whereas the present Congregation, after expending all the Subscriptions, Loans, Gifts, &c., made the Society by themselves, & the generous Patrons, of their religious Intentions to the amount of at least £2200 were obliged to borrow Money to finish the Buildings & contract other Debts that is now not only pressingly claim'd but a Judgment, will actually be obtained against their House of Worship, which must be sold unless they are speedily enabled to pay the sum of about £800 - And which from a Variety of delicate & distressing Causes they are wholly unable to raise among themselves. They are therefore under the necessity of earnestly soliciting from their worthy fellow Citizens of every religious Denomination, their benevolent Aid & Help flattering themselves that their worshipping Almighty God in a way & manner different from other religious Societies, will never deter the enlightened Citizens of Philadelphia, from generously subscribing towards the preservation of a religious house of Worship. The subscription paper, will be enrolled, in the Archives of their Congregation, that their Posterity may know, & gratefully remember the liberal Supporters of their religious Society.

21. A Declaration of Synagogue Rights - ca. 1790

This "declaration of rights" was promulgated by members of Congre-
gation Shearith Israel in New York, when they rewrote their constitution
in the wake of the Revolution. The language of the document, echoing
that of the Constitution, as well as the democratic nature of the rights
themselves, demonstrates the impact of American ideals even on internal
synagogue life.

Whereas in free states all power originates and is derived from the
people, who always retain every right necessary for their well being
individually, and, for the better ascertaining those rights with more
precision and explicitly, frequently from [form?] a declaration or bill of
those rights. In like manner the individuals of every society in such
state are entitled to and retain their several rights, which ought to be
preserved inviolate.

Therefore we, the profession [professors] of the Divine Laws,
members of this holy congregation of Shearith Israel, in the city of New
York, conceive it our duty to make this declaration of our rights and
previleges, *vizt.:*

First, of Jews in general. That every free person professing the
Jewish religion, and who lives according to its holy precepts, is entitled
to worship the God of Israel in the synagogue, and by purchase or gift
to have a seat therein, and to be treated in all respect as a brother, and
as such a subject of every fraternal duty.

Secondly. Of those who have been for a length of time members of
the K.K., though not reputed *yehidim* ["members"]: That all those who
have formerly and now continue to be members of this *kahal kodosh*
["holy congregation"] at large, not having subscribed to the constitutions of the aforesaid congregation, but living as worthy professors of
our holy law, are entitled to the several privileges in the foregoing articles, and shall be called to *sepher* [the reading of the "Scroll"] when not
interfering with the [prior] rights of a *yahid.*

Thirdly. Of the *yehidim*: The qualifications of the *yehidim* being
defined in the constitution, reference is to be had thereto.

Of Their Rights

[Firstly.] They are entitled to all the privileges in the preceding
articles.

Secondly. Every *yahid* is entitled to vote for the adjuntas and for
the several officers and servants of the congregations, according to the
mode prescribed in the aforesaid constitution. However, as this is a
right, it by no means obliges either their attendance at a junto [congre-
gational meeting?] or to vote, it being at their own option.

Thirdly. Any *yahid* who is desirous of having a copy of the constitution aforesaid may have one.

Fourthly. In ordinary, to have the preference of being called to *sepher* and in all the *metzvots* [religious honors].

Fifthly. When a *yahid* has a son born, he shall have the distribution of the *metzvots* the Sabbath preceding the *berit* ["circumcision"], provided it be to such as may by the constitution be lawfull; and if he has a daughter born, he shall be called to *sepher* the Sabbat after, and if he acquaints the acting parnas in time, he shall be also called to *sepher* on the [first] day his wife comes to synagogue [after she has given birth].

Sixthly. In case of death in his family, the *hazan* ["cantor"] and *shamas* ["beadle"] shall attend the funeral at the place appointed, provided the *shamas* has due notice given him (whose duty is to acquaint the *hazan*), and, if requested, the *hazan* shall mention in synagogue the time of the funeral, the place of meeting at and after the funeral, the *hazan* to perform the usual duties of his function.

Seventhly. In case of the marriage of a *yahid* or any of his family, the *hazan* shall officiate, and the *hatan* [bridegroom] shall have the distribution of all the *metzvot* the Sabbath next ensuing said marriage, to such persons as by the constitution it is permitted, and provided also that the marriage is consonant to our holy law, and the persons concerned be not under any disqualification otherways by the constitution.

Eightly. Every *yahid* is entitled to be chosen *hatan torah* ["bridegroom of the Law"] or *hatan bershit* ["bridegroom of Genesis"], and those who have been before [this in the office of] either of the *hattanim*, or paid their fine for non acceptance, are entitled to be chosen parnassim, and such as have served as parnas or adjunto may be elected to any of the before mentioned offices, subject nevertheless to the penalties for non acceptance as declared in the constitution.

Ninthly. In all general meetings . . . or any other usual meetings, every *yahid* has and ought to have a right of debating on any subject whatsoever with decency, yet to deliver his sentiments without restraint, and freely to give his opinions and advice concerning any matters in question, or to open a new subject in order, at his own option.

Tenthly. That every *yahid* has and ought to have a right to make his offering in synagogue in the Hebrew language or in the Portugese, and in those languages only (the latter having been practiced from the establishment of this congregation), as he shall think proper to do, and this article to extend to all and every person who makes this *misheberach* or offering, but always avoiding any thing satirical, offensive, or otherways indecent.

Elevently. If any number of *yehidim* (not less than three) have any thing to propose to a general junta ["meeting"], the parnasim and adjuntas are to be applied to, and if they are desirous of a general junta to be called, and they adduce sufficient reason for it, the parnas shall summon such general meetings as soon after as may be convenient. . . .

22. *A Guarantee for Paul Revere - 1789*

This letter of introduction and personal guarantee was provided by Moses Michael Hays (1739-1805) to the famous Boston patriot, Paul Revere. Having sided with the forces of independence (see Chapter II, Documents 3 and 4), Hays fled Newport, going first to Philadelphia and later to Boston, where he prospered and became a prominent Mason. He befriended Paul Revere (later appointing him his deputy grand master in the Massachusetts Grand Lodge), and attempted to help him, in this case unsuccessfully, to obtain iron for his foundry.

Boston, 9th September, 1789.

Messrs. Brown & Benson,
Providence.

Gentlemen:

Colonel Paul Revere will hand you this. His business to Providence is to purchase five or six tons of pig metal, which he wishes to have at three or four months credit, understanding that it is the usual terms you sell pig metal. Colonel Revere will punctually comply with his contract for such a quantity, and for which I will by this letter be his guarantee.

I am with respect, gentlemen,

Your humble servant,
M.M. Hays

23. Rebecca Samuel Writes Home - 1791

This historically valuable family letter, translated here from the original Yiddish, portrays some of the social and religious challenges which post-war mobility posed for American Jews. Quite incidentally, it also demonstrates early attitudes toward Jews who arrived in America as part of the German Hessian forces, originally brought over by England to fight rebellious colonists.

Petersburg, January 12, 1791, Wednesday, 8th [7th?] Shebat, 5551.
Dear and Worthy Parents:

I received your dear letter with much pleasure and therefrom understand that you are in good health, thank God, and that made us especially happy. The same is not lacking with us - may we live to be a hundred years. Amen.

Dear parents, you complain that you do not receive any letters from us, and my mother-in-law writes the same. I don't know what's going on. I have written more letters than I have received from you. Whenever I can and have an opportunity, I give letters to take along, and I send letters by post when I do not have any other opportunity. It is already six months since we received letters from you and from London. The last letter you sent was through Sender [Alexander], and it was the beginning of the month of Ab [July, 1790] when we received it. Now you can realize that we too have been somewhat worried. We are completely isolated here. We do not have any friends, and when we do not hear from you for any length of time, it is enough to make us sick. I hope that I will get to see some of my family. That will give me some satisfaction.

You write me that Mr. Jacob Renner's son Reuben is in Philadelphia and that he will come to us. People will not advise him to come to Virginia. When the Jews of Philadelphia or New York hear the name Virginia, they get nasty. And they are not wrong! It won't do for a Jew. In the first place it is an unhealthful district, and we are only human. God forbid, if anything should happen to us, where would we be thrown? There is no cemetery in the whole of Virginia. In Richmond, which is twenty-two miles from here, there is a Jewish community consisting of two quorums [twenty men], and the two cannot muster a quarter [quorum when needed?].

You cannot imagine what kinds of Jews they have here [in Virginia]. They were all German itinerants who made a living by begging in Germany. They came to America during the war, as soldiers, and now they can't recognize themselves.

One can make a good living here, and all live at peace. Anyone can do what he wants. There is no rabbi in all of America to excommunicate anyone. This is a blessing here; Jew and Gentile are as one. There is no *galut* ["exile," rejection of Jews] here. In New York and Philadelphia there is more *galut*. The reason is that there are too many German Gentiles and Jews there. The German Gentiles cannot forsake their anti-Jewish prejudice; and the German Jews cannot forsake their disgraceful conduct; and that's what makes the *galut*.

[Rebecca Samuel]

Barrak Hays - New York soldier who served with the British Loyalist Forces, and later settled in Canada.

Isaac Franks House in Germantown, Pa. - George Washington used this house as the temporary capital in 1793 during the yellow fever epidemic.

Moses Michael Hays - 18th century Boston merchant, banker, and
Masonic leader. (See Documents 3, 22.)

The prayerbook of Solomon Bush and his mother, Rebecca, dated May 10, 1785 - Solomon Bush was the only Jewish combat soldier who attained the rank of Lt. Colonel during the American Revolution. He was severely wounded in the Battle of Brandywine in 1777. (See Document 8.)

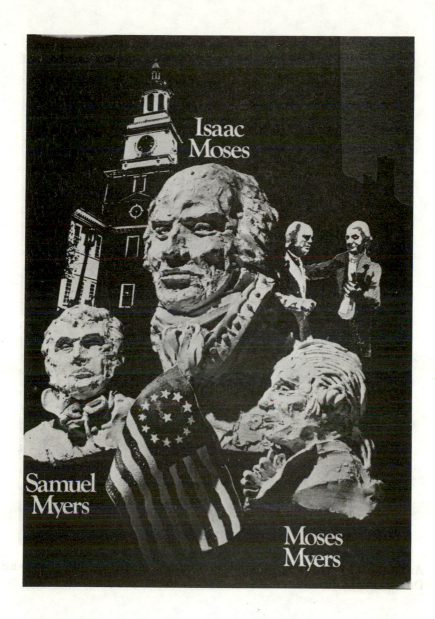

Isaac
Moses

Samuel
Myers

Moses
Myers

Aaron Lopez - Newport merchant and shipper. (See Chapter 2 and Document 10.)

David S. Franks - Colonial merchant who served as an officer in the Revolutionary forces, and was later granted four hundred acres of land as a reward.

Isaac Moses - Leading New York merchant and Revolutionary activist. Helped provide the Revolutionary forces with money and materials. (See Document 11.)

Haym Salomon - Bicentennial commemorative postage stamp. The Revolutionary broker and patriot was honored by the United States Postal Service in a series entitled "Contributors to the Cause." (See Documents 15, 16.)

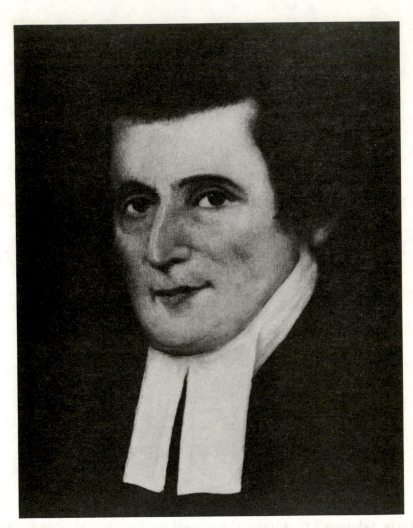

Gershom Mendes Seixas - Minister of Congregation Shearith Israel. He sided with the Revolutionary forces, and fled New York in the wake of British occupation. (See Documents 2, 18.)

Mordecai Sheftall - Savannah merchant and early opponent of British rule. Member of a prominent family of patriots. (See Documents 1, 9, 13, 17.)

Isaac Touro - Minister of the Newport Jewish Congregation. During the Revolution he sided with the British, and later left the Colonies for Kingston, Jamaica. His son, Judah Touro, was a prominent New Orleans merchant and, in his later years, a leading philanthropist.

CHAPTER V

THE NEW NATION AND THE JEWS

The Declaration of Independence, followed shortly thereafter by the ratification of the Constitution (1787) and the Bill of Rights (1791), has frequently been viewed as a watershed in Jewish history. Never before had a country so completely committed itself to religious liberty, separating church from state on the one hand, while on the other it guaranteed free exercise of religion to all believers whatever their creed. In Europe, Jews needed to await specific legislation guaranteeing them their rights. In America, by contrast, consideration of what would later be known as the "Jewish question" almost never intruded into debates over the Constitution. For the most part, Jews won their rights as a matter of course, along with members of all other minority religions.

The situation differed on the state level where in some cases Christianity (usually Protestantism) continued to receive official sanction, and Jews, among others, were still denied the right to hold civil offices - a situation maintained in Maryland until 1826 and in New Hampshire all the way up until 1877. Even when Jews did receive legal equality, that by no means automatically translated into social equality. Indeed, manifestations of anti-Judaism continued to occur periodically. The great promise of America did nevertheless have an enormous impact on Jewish life, for henceforward religious bigotry could properly be condemned as "un-American." Though Americans sometimes strayed from the principles for which the Founding Fathers contended, the country's fundamental laws and ideals relating to religious freedom remained unchanged.

HOW AMERICAN JEWS ACQUIRED POLITICAL RIGHTS

Oscar and Mary Handlin

In this article, the Handlins survey "the consequences of indepen-
dence" in terms of the acquisition by American Jews of their political
rights. They analyze federal and state developments affecting Jews, and
place them in their historical context, pointing out as they do that the last
traces of religious establishment - state-enforced Christianity - all but
disappeared in the United States by the third decade of the nineteenth
century. But vestiges of the old order continued far longer, and Jews con-
tinued on the alert, vigilant lest their hard-won gains be lost.

Several distinct strands entered into the achievement of American independence. The Revolution involved, in the first instance, a total separation from England. But the break entailed also the destruction of an ancient system of authority; and that called for justification. The Americans who were pulling down an empire were anxious also to establish a nation. They felt the compulsion to set forth the reasonable, orderly, legal grounds for their actions. They based their thinking on the conceptions of natural rights and law derived from the Enlightenment and from the heritage of their own experience. And the intellectual revolution that ensued had profound implications for the general relationships between church and state and also for the position of the Jews in the United States.

The logic of the Revolution had elevated reason above tradition and the natural rights of the individual above constituted authority. It was no longer possible to regard the established church as other than an outmoded vestige of the past. The theory in the Declaration of Independence explained what Americans had already learned in practice, that religious faith involved an exercise of individual choice in which the state ought not to interfere.

Furthermore, in most parts of the continent the established church was a vestige of the imperial connection - the Church of England - and vulnerable on that account alone. Earlier, while they were still colonists, Americans had resisted the establishment of an episcopate that would tie them further to Britain. Now citizens of an independent nation, such a link was still more abhorrent. The fact that the Anglican clergy had generally been loyal to the Crown and had resisted the Revolution was additional evidence of the necessity of dissolving the established church, indeed of divorcing entirely the church from the state.

The decisive steps came in Virginia. As the states, each in turn, came to frame a constitution, they were most likely to seek a model in that of the Old Dominion where so many of the great leaders of the

Revolution were at home. What happened in Virginia therefore was important far beyond its own borders, indeed far beyond the borders of the United States.

The first test came quickly in 1776 as the Virginia state constitutional convention considered a Bill of Rights. At the urging of James Madison, a clause providing for the fullest toleration in the exercise of religion was rejected. In its stead, the Bill of Rights proclaimed, "All men are equally entitled to the free exercise of religion according to the dictates of conscience." The emphasis was not upon *toleration* merely, but upon the equality of all sects.

The position of the Virginia churches remained ambiguous for some years, however. No state grants were made to the Anglican Church; such grants no doubt were contrary to the intent of the Bill of Rights. But it was an open question as to whether the Bill also precluded equal grants by the state to all the recognized sects. That might leave the way open for the establishment of Christianity, rather than any form of it, as the established religion. Thus, in 1784 a bill proposed to tax every citizen for the support "of some Christian church."

Once more Madison was moved to action. "Who does not see," he asked, "that the same authority which can establish Christianity to the exclusion of all other religions may establish, with the same ease, any particular sect of Christians in exclusion of all other sects?" His opposition helped defeat the proposal and, with Jefferson, he secured the enactment of the statute establishing religious liberty. That law was deliberately phrased broadly enough to comprehend the Jew. Believing that "the reason of man may be trusted with the formation of his own opinions," the Virginians had completely severed the ties between church and state.

From Virginia the principle was rapidly extended to other states and to the Federal government. The Pennsylvania constitution of 1776 and the New York constitution of 1777 called for religious equality. The Northwest Ordinance adopted by the Continental Congress in 1787 set forth the same principle. Article VI of the new constitution of the United States forbade any religious test for national office; and the first amendment, Article I of the Bill of Rights, prevented Congress from making any law "respecting an establishment of religion, or prohibiting the free exercise thereof." The purpose of these constitutional barriers was, as Jefferson put it, to build "a wall of separation between Church and State."

By and large, progress in these terms, by 1790, justified the tone of self-congratulation in which George Washington and the various Jewish congregations of the country greeted one another. All Americans, the first President pointed out, in August 1790, "possess alike liberty of conscience and immunities of citizenship. It is now no more that toleration is spoken of, as if it was by the indulgence of one class of people, that another enjoyed the exercise of their inherent natural rights. For happily the government of the United States, which gives to bigotry no sanction, to persecution no assistance, requires only that they who live under its protection should demean themselves as good citizens, in giving it on all occasions their effectual support."

The President's assertion was slightly exaggerated. In a few respects, Jews still suffered from disabilities that were the products of surviving traces of establishment in some of the states. Those disabilities were slower to disappear.

The development of the principle of separation had been slowest in New England. Their distinctive role gave the established churches a longer life there than in the rest of the nation. The Congregationalists had not been tainted with an English connection. Indeed, many ministers had been in the forefront of the Revolution and had thus acquired patriotic status. Moving toward liberal, often Unitarian or Universalist, affiliations, they were also in accord with the spirit of the times. The dissolution of the ties between church and state was therefore more gradual in New England, particularly since here the number of Jews and other dissenters was relatively small.

Moreover, although full separation of church and state was not yet achieved, the discriminatory consequences had already been substantially eliminated or mitigated. The members of churches other than the orthodox were allowed to direct their taxes to be appropriated to the use of the ministers or the religious institutions of their own denominations. This tolerance extended to the Jews, as to others. Thus in 1808 Moses Michael Hays appeared before the magistrates of the City of Boston and declared that he was a member of a synagogue of the Jews, and ought not to be taxed to support the Congregational Church.

With time and with the appearance of schismatic divisions among the Congregationalists, establishment became ever less meaningful. One state after another took the inescapable road to disestablishment. By the 1830's the process was complete; Massachusetts, the last state to act, divorced church from state in 1833. A rear-guard action by conservatives like Joseph Story who wished to substitute a general establishment of Christianity for the particular establishment of any sect failed as it had failed almost fifty years earlier in Virginia. The trend was irresistible. In the process, the religious equality of the Jew was made legally complete. Their congregations were eligible for incorporation and treated in law like the associations of every other sect.

The religious disabilities under which the Jews suffered after 1833 were not explicitly directed against them, but were rather the indirect result of vestiges of older practice left in law. Although the general attitude toward Jews was friendly, public opinion often was slow in rectifying these discriminatory features.

In some of the states, for instance, the formula for oaths included references to belief in the Trinity or the New Testament, to which Jews could not conscientiously subscribe. Several such oaths - as for jurors or witnesses - were altered with little difficulty. But now and again, a more serious problem arose with regard to the oaths required of the holders of elective office.

By the end of the Revolution, Jews had been chosen not only to local posts in some cities, but had also been selected for more responsible positions in many parts of the country. There was no inclination to bar these people from public office and generally the question of the offensive oaths had only to be raised to be resolved. Thus the Jews of Philadelphia, in 1783-84, protested as a "stigma upon their nation and religion" the requirement that members of the General Assembly take an oath affirming belief in the New Testament. The revised constitution of Pennsylvania, a few years later, explicitly barred the disqualification on account of religious sentiments of any person "who acknowledges the being of a God and a future state of rewards and punishments."

In states like Maryland and North Carolina, however, where the number of Jews was small, the issue was not systematically raised by any organized community. The oaths remained in use unnoticed, unquestioned until the election of some Jewish official or the conscientious scrutiny of some Christian legislator unexpectedly brought the matter into the open. Then emotional obstacles sometimes temporarily stood in the way of the logical solution. But such obstacles rarely were strong enough to perpetuate injustice, nor did they long delay the trend toward equality.

Thus, in 1809, Jacob Henry, reelected to the North Carolina House of Commons, found the right to his seat challenged because he was a Jew who would not take an oath affirming the divine character of the New Testament. After a spirited defense, Henry was nevertheless permitted to keep his seat; a legal subterfuge made it possible for him to do so without a change in the requirement. Traces of the old provisions lingered in North Carolina until they were completely eliminated by the state constitution of 1868.

A similar test in Maryland extended over a long period and evoked a penetrating discussion that clarified the most significant issues involved.

The Maryland constitution of 1776 had made "a declaration of a belief in the Christian religion" requisite to holding office. A petition by the Jews in 1797 for relief from this provision had been found reasonable by the House of Delegates, but had led to no concrete measure of relief.

The question was raised again in 1818 by Thomas Kennedy, a Scotch Presbyterian immigrant and member of the legislature, who took up the cudgels on behalf of the Jews out of a sense of the injustice of the legal position to which they had been relegated. Year after year he introduced his bill to give them equality of status and thus to extirpate the remnants of the prejudice of centuries, until he was finally successful in 1826. His own interests were purely altruistic, representing as he did a constituency entirely without Jews. He was moved, as other Americans were, by a consciousness that religious equality and the separation of church and state were among the proudest achievements of the Republic. "America," he said, "has wisely relinquished it to the insidious policy of regal governments, to make an instrument of religion," by having "forever sundered the spiritual from the temporal concerns of men."

As the second third of the century opened, the last traces of establishment had all but disappeared in the United States. The way was then open for a further struggle to explore some of the social consequences of the new relationship between government and religion. In many spheres of American life that exploration would call forth an effort to give new and greater depth to the conception of equality.

SOURCE: Oscar and Mary Handlin, "The Acquisition of Political and Social Rights by the Jews in the United States," *American Jewish Year Book* 56 (1955), pp. 54-58. Reprinted by permission of the *American Jewish Year Book*.

*24. North Carolina Disestablishes Religion,
But Maintains Protestantism Secure - 1776*

*The North Carolina State Constitution, rewritten in the wake of
Independence, is typical of several early state moves toward religious
freedom. While it abolished all forms of religious establishment, and
dropped other forms of religious coercion, it still continued to exclude all
non-Protestants from "holding any office or place of trust or profit in the
civil department within this State."*

Article XXXI. That no clergyman, or preacher of the gospel, of any
denomination, shall be capable of being a member of either the Senate,
House of Commons, or Council of State, while he continues in the exercise of the pastoral function.

Article XXXII. That no person, who shall deny the being of God or
the truth of the Protestant religion, or the divine authority either of
the Old or New Testaments, or who shall hold religious principles
incompatible with the freedom and safety of the State, shall be capable
of holding any office or place of trust or profit in the civil department
within this State.

Article XXXIV. That there shall be no establishment of any one
religious church or denomination in this State, in preference to any
other; neither shall any person, on any pretence whatsoever, be compelled to attend any place of worship contrary to his own faith or judgment, nor be obliged to pay, for the purchase of any glebe, or the
building of any house of worship, or for the maintenance of any minister or ministry, contrary to what he believes right, or has voluntarily
and personally engaged to perform; but all persons shall be at liberty
to exercise their own mode of worship: *Provided*, That nothing herein
contained shall be construed to exempt preachers of treasonable or
seditious discourses, from legal trial and punishment.

25. *"Free Exercise and Enjoyment of Religion" in New York - 1777*

The New York State Constitution of 1777 took a most imporant step toward effecting American religious liberty, and displays the impact of the ideological currents of the day. Without saying so explicitly, it offered Jews complete religious equality, the first state constitution to do so. The last clause in the article nevertheless left the door open to certain restrictions, which were in fact promulgated, especially against Catholics.

The New York State Constitution of 1777

Article XXXVIII

And whereas we are required, by the benevolent principles of rational liberty, not only to expel civil tyranny, but also to guard against that spiritual oppression and intolerance wherewith the bigotry and ambition of weak and wicked priests and princes have scourged mankind, this convention doth further, in the name and by the authority of the good people of this state, ordain, determine, and declare, that the free exercise and enjoyment of religious profession and worship, without discrimination or preference, shall forever hereafter be allowed, within this state, to all mankind; *provided,* that the liberty of conscience, hereby granted, shall not be so construed as to excuse acts of licentiousness, or justify practices inconsistent with the peace or safety of this state.

26. Philadelphia Jews Appeal for Civil Rights - 1783

Jewish notables in Philadelphia appealed to their state's Council of Censors in 1783 asking it to alter laws forcing members of the state house of representatives to acknowledge the divinity of the New Testament. The offending measure was not deleted until a new Pennsylvania constitution was promulgated in 1790.

[December, 1783.]

To the honourable, the Council of Censors, assembled agreeable to the constitution of the State of Pennsylvania.

The memorial of Rabbi Ger. Seixas of the synagogue of the Jews at Philadelphia, Simon Nathan, their *parnass* or president, Asher Myers, Bernard Gratz, and Haym Salomon, the *mahamad*, or associates of their council, in behalf of themselves and their bretheren Jews, residing in Pennsylvania, most respectfully sheweth:

That by the tenth section of the Frame of Government of this commonwealth [adopted in 1776], it is ordered that each member of the general assembly of representatives of the freemen of Pennsylvania, before he takes his seat, shall make and subscribe a declaration which ends in these words, "I do acknowledge the Scriptures of the Old and New Testament to be given by divine inspiration," to which is added an assurance that "no further or other religious test shall ever hereafter be required of any civil officer or magistrate in this state."

Your memorialists beg leave to observe that this clause seems to limit the civil rights of your citizens to one very special article of the creed, whereas, by the second paragraph of the declaration of the rights of the inhabitants, it is asserted without any other limitation than the professing the existence of God, in plain words, "that no man who acknowledges the being of a God can be justly deprived or abridged of any civil rights as a citizen on account of his religious sentiments." But certainly this religious test deprives the Jews of the most eminent rights of freemen, solemnly ascertained to all men who are not professed atheists.

May it please your Honors: Although the Jews in Pennsylvania are but few in number, yet liberty of the people in one country, and the declaration of the government thereof, that these liberties are the rights of the people, may prove a powerful attractive to men who live under restraints in another country. Holland and England have made valuable acquisitions of men, who, for their religious sentiments, were distressed in their own countries.

And if Jews in Europe or elsewhere should incline to transport themselves to America, and would, for reason of some certain advantage of the soil, climate, or the trade of Pennsylvania, rather become inhabitants thereof, than of any other state, yet the disability of Jews to take seat among the representatives of the people, as worded by the said religious test, might determine their free choice to go to New-York, or to any other of the United States of America, where there is no such like restraint laid upon the nation and religion of the Jews, as in Pennsylvania.

Your memorialists cannot say that the Jews are particularly fond of being representatives of the people in assembly or civil officers and magistrates in the state, but with great submission they apprehend that a clause in the constitution, which disables them to be elected by their fellow citizens to represent them in assembly, as [is] a stigma upon their nation and their religion, and it is inconsonant with the second paragraph of the said bill of rights. Otherwise, Jews are as fond of liberty as other religious societies can be, and it must create in them a displeasure when they perceive that for their professed dissent to a doctrine, which is inconsistent with their religious sentiments, they should be excluded from the most important and honourable part of the rights of a free citizen.

Your memorialists beg farther leave to represent that in the religious books of the Jews, which are or may be in every man's hands, there are no such doctrines or principles established as are inconsistent with the safety and happiness of the people of Pennsylvania, and that the conduct and behaviour of the Jews in this and the neighbouring states has always tallied with the great design of the Revolution; [they beg farther leave to represent] that the Jews of Charlestown, New-York, New-Port, and other posts occupied by the British troops, have distinguishedly suffered for their attachment to the Revolution principles; and their brethren at St. Eustatius, for the same cause, experienced the most severe resentments of the British commanders.

The Jews of Pennsylvania, in proportion to the number of their members, can count with any religious society whatsoever the Whigs [the patriots] among either of them. They have served some of them in the Continental army; some went out in the militia to fight the common enemy; all of them have chearfully contributed to the support of the militia and of the government of this state.

They have no inconsiderable property in lands and tenements, but particularly in the way of trade, some more, some less, for which they pay taxes. They have, upon every plan formed for public utility, been forward to contribute as much as their circumstances would admit of, and as a nation or a religious society, they stand unimpeached of any matter whatsoever against the safety and happiness of the people.

And your memorialists humbly pray that if your honours, from any other consideration than the subject of this address, should think proper to call a convention for revising the constitution, you would be pleased to recommend this to the notice of that convention.

27. Shearith Israel Welcomes George Clinton Home - 1784

This address welcoming back Governor George Clinton of New York from his period in exile illustrates both the patriotic piety of New York Jews and their hopes for the future. It was sent following Congregation Shearith Israel's first official meeting after its own return from exile, and was signed by the congregation's three most distinguished patriots.

[New York, January, 1784.]

To His Excellency, George Clinton, Esquire, Governor, Captain General, and Commander in Chief of the Militia of the State of New York, and Admiral of the Navy of the Same: May it please your Excellency:

We, the members of the antient congregation of Israelites, lately returned from exile, beg leave to welcome your arrival in this city with our most cordial congratulations.

Though the society we belong to is but small when compared with other religious societies, yet we flatter ourselves that none has manifested a more zealous attachment to the sacred cause of America in the late war with Great Britain.

We derive, therefore, the highest satisfaction from reflecting that it pleased the Almighty Arbiter of Events to dispose us to take part with the country we lived in; and we now look forward with pleasure to the happy days we expect to enjoy under a constitution wisely framed to preserve the inestimable blessings of civil and religious liberty.

Taught by our Divine Legislator to obey our rulers, and prompted thereto by the dictates of our own reason, it will be the anxious endeavour of the members of our congregation to render themselves worthy of these blessings by discharging the duties of good citizens, and, as an inviolable regard to justice and the constitution has ever distinguished your administration, they rest confident of receiving an equal share of your patronage.

May the Supreme Governor of the Universe take you under His holy protection, and may you long continue to exercise the dignified office you now possess, with honor to yourself and advantage to your constituents.

We have the honor to be, with the greatest respect in behalf of the antient congregation of Israelites,
Your Excellency's very obedient humble servants,
[Hayman Levy, Myer Myers, Isaac Moses.]

28. The Northwest Ordinance - 1787

The Northwest Ordinance of 1787 laid the groundwork for subsequent Constitutional attitudes toward religion. On the one hand, it guaranteed both free exercise of religion and the right to have no religion. On the other hand, it explicitly included religion among things "necessary to good government and the happiness of mankind."

AN ORDINANCE

FOR THE GOVERNMENT OF THE TERRITORY OF THE UNITED STATES NORTHWEST OF THE RIVER OHIO

Adopted in the Continental Congress, July 13, 1787.

ARTICLE I.

No person demeaning himself in a peaceable and orderly manner, shall ever be molested on account of his mode of worship or religious sentiments in the said territory.

ARTICLE II.

Religion, morality, and knowledge being necessary to good government and the happiness of mankind, schools and the means of education shall forever be encouraged.

29. For a Protestant America - 1788

This excerpt from an article entitled "Anti-Federalist, No. 1" (February 8, 1788) opposing New Hampshire's ratification of the Constitution, presents the case for limited religious liberty, arguing that America should be ruled only by Protestants. While this anti-Federalist view never commanded a majority, it continued to find adherents long after the Constitution had come into effect.

Upon the discarding of all religious tests, Art. 6, clause 3 - But no religious test shall ever be required as a qualification to any office, or public trust under the United States, according to this we may have a Papist, a Mohomatan, a Deist, yea an Atheist at the helm of Government; all nations are tenatious of their religion, and all have an acknowledgement of it in their civil establishment; but the new plan requires none at all; none in Congress, none in any member of the legislative bodies; none in any single officer of the United States; all swept off at one stroke totally contrary to our state plans. - But will this be good policy to discard all religion? It may be said the meaning is not to discard it, but only to shew that there is no need of it in public officers; they may be as faithful without as with - this is a mistake - when a man has no regard to God and his laws nor any belief of a future state; he will have less regard to the laws of men, or to the most solemn oaths or affirmations; it is acknowledged by all that civil governments can't well be supported without the assistance of religion; I think therefore that so much deference ought to be paid to it, as to acknowledge it in our civil establishment; and that no man is fit to be a ruler of protestants, without he can honestly profess to be of the protestant religion.

30. The Federal Parade and the "Separate Table for the Jews" - 1788

The recollections contained in this letter sent by Naphtali Phillips (1773-1870) to John McAllister, Jr., and dated October 24, 1868, describe the Federal parade of 1788 honoring ratification of the Constitution. As the document relates, Jews both took part in the ceremony and remained apart from it, eating at special kosher tables.

New York, October 24th, 1868

My dear friend, McAllister:

My good grandson is now at my elvow and would have been before had his business allowed him time.

When I wrote you in a former letter respecting "Bartram's Garden" [for botany, on the Schuylkill] little did I expect the pleasure received by your letter and accompanying pamphlet. Please make my respects to the present incumbent of the garden, and hope he will realize all your expectations in relation thereto.

As it respects the great Federal procession in "1788," I have been anticipated by the *Sunday Dispatch*. I shall make a few particulars in addition thereto.

First, in an open carriage, drawn by elegant horses, sat Chief Justice McKane [Thomas McKean], with other judges of the [Pennsylvania] Supreme Court, holding in his hand the new constitution in a frame. This was received by the populace with great rejoicing. I do not think I can give the procession in its particular order, but I give it to you as well as I recollect. Then came farmers with large cattle and sheep on a platform drawn by horses, all handsomely decorated. The farmers were sowing grain as they walked along. Then came an handsome ship elegantly adorned with flags in all parts of it, manned by young midshipmen and drawn by horses, on wheels, and one of the crew throwing the lead as they passed along singing out in true sailors' voice "by the deep nine, quarter less seven," and so on.

Next a printing press on a platform drawn by horses, compositors, setting types, and the press worked by journeymen distributing some printed matter as they went along.

Speaking of the press, brings to my mind the words of "Junius," as follows: "Let it be impressed on your minds, let it be instilled to your children, that the liberty of the press is a great palladium of your civil and religious rights." I do not know that I have given you the exact words, but you have the substance.

Next came the blacksmiths with their forge, with a large bellows keeping up a blast to keep alive the flame of liberty. Next came shoemakers on a platform, men and boys soleing and heeltapping, others making wax ends [for sewing shoes]. Then followed three fine-looking men dressed in black velvet with large wigs on, densely powdered, representing the hairdressing society. Then the various trades followed with their appropriate insignia; young lads from different schools lead by their ministers and teachers, of which I was one of the boys.

The procession then proceeded from about Third Street near Spruce, northward towards Callowhill Street, then wheeled towards Bush Hill, where there was a number of long tables loaded with all kinds of provisions, with a separate table for the Jews, who could not partake of the meats from the other tables; but they had a full supply of soused [pickled] salmon, bread and crackers, almonds, raisins, etc. This table was under the charge of an old cobbler named Isaac Moses, well known in Philadelphia at that time. There was no spiritous liquer for the company. Having doon [done] full justice to the good things provided for, the procession then retrograded. It was the last I saw of them.

I reached home late in the afternoon, fatigued and hungry; my kind, good parents having provided a good meal for me. I retired to rest and knew nothing till I saw the sun shining in my room the next morning.

Sometime after the procession, a large sign was exhibited at some public house representing the federal convention members, all being present as they sat with Gen'l Washington at their head as their president, and at the lower part of the sign were these words: "These thirty-seven great men together have agreed that better times shall soon succeed." So ends the procession.

31. The First Amendment - 1789

The First Amendment to the Constitution of the United States, passed by Congress on September 25, 1789, was ratified, along with the other nine amendments that comprise the Bill of Rights, on December 15, 1791. The amendment has served as the legal basis for religious freedom and church-state separation in America. Although originally limited in its application only to laws passed by Congress, all states eventually enacted similar guarantees. The Supreme Court ruled in the 1940s that, under the Fourteenth Amendment, First Amendment liberties apply to laws passed by state legislatures as well.

AMENDMENT I

Congress shall make no law respecting an establishment of religion, or prohibiting the free exercise thereof; or abridging the freedom of speech or of the press; or the right of the people peaceably to assemble, and to petition the government for a redress of grievances.

32. Newport Jews Welcome President George Washington - 1790

This document and the next (Document 33), the correspondence between Newport Jews and President George Washington, are among the most famous documents in American Jewish history. The address to Washington was occasioned by his visit to Newport in August, 1790. The President's formal reply, sent sometime later, echoed themes sounded in the address, and emphasized Jewish rights and liberties. Washington exchanged similar letters with other Jewish communities.

To the President of the United States of America,
Sir:

Permit the children of the stock of Abraham to approach you with the most cordial affection and esteem for your person and merits and to join with our fellow-citizens in welcoming you to New Port.

With pleasure we reflect on those days - those days of difficulty and danger - when the God of Israel who delivered David from the peril of the sword shielded your head in the day of battle. And we rejoice to think that the same Spirit, who rested in the bosom of the greatly beloved Daniel, enabling him to preside over the provinces of the Babylonish Empire, rests, and ever will rest upon you, enabling you to discharge the arduous duties of Chief Magistrate in these states.

Deprived as we have hitherto been of the invaluable rights of free citizens, we now, with a deep sense of gratitude to the Almighty Disposer of all events, behold a government, erected by the majesty of the people, a government which to bigotry gives no sanction, to persecution no assistance, but generously affording to all liberty of conscience and immunities of citizenship, deeming every one, of whatever nation, tongue, or language, equal parts of the great governmental machine. This so ample and extensive federal union whose basis is philanthropy, mutual confidence, and public virtue, we cannot but acknowledge to be the work of the Great God, who ruleth in the armies of heaven and among the inhabitants of the earth, doing whatsoever seemeth him good.

For all the blessings of civil and religious liberty which we enjoy under an equal and benign administration, we desire to send up our thanks to the Antient of Days, the great Preserver of Men, beseeching him that the angel who conducted our forefathers through the wilderness into the promised land may graciously conduct you through all the dangers and difficulties of this mortal life. And when like Joshua, full of days and full of honor, you are gathered to your fathers, may you be admitted into the heavenly paradise to partake of the water of life and the tree of immortality.

Done and signed by order of the Hebrew Congregation in New Port, Rhode Island, August 17th, 1790.

Moses Seixas, Warden

33. George Washington Replies to the Hebrew Congregation in Newport - 1790

Of all George Washington's letters to Jews, this is the best known, for it employs the oft-cited phrase "to bigotry no sanction, to persecution no assistance." While Washington actually borrowed this phrase from the original letter sent to him by the Newport Jews (Document 32), the context here is somewhat different. Washington stresses that Jews are entitled to more than simple "toleration" in America, for their religious liberty is based upon "inherent natural rights."

To the Hebrew Congregation in New Port, Rhode Island,

Gentlemen:

While I receive with much satisfaction your address replete with expressions of affection and esteem, I rejoice in the opportunity of assuring you that I shall always retain a grateful remembrance of the cordial welcome I experienced in my visit to New Port from all classes of citizens.

The reflection on the days of difficulty and danger which are past is rendered the more sweet from a consciousness that they are succeeded by days of uncommon prosperity and security. If we have wisdom to make the best use of the advantages with which we are now favored, we cannot fail, under the just administration of a good government, to become a great and a happy people.

The citizens of the United States of America have a right to applaud themselves for having given to mankind examples of an enlarged and liberal policy, a policy worthy of imitation.

All possess alike liberty of conscience and immunities of citizenship. It is now no more that toleration is spoken of, as if it was by the indulgence of one class of people that another enjoyed the exercise of their inherent natural rights. For happily the government of the United States, which gives to bigotry no sanction, to persecution no assistance, requires only that they who live under its protection should demean themselves as good citizens, in giving it on all occasions their effectual support.

It would be inconsistent with the frankness of my character not to avow that I am pleased with your favorable opinion of my administration and fervent wishes for my felicity.

May the children of the stock of Abraham who dwell in this land continue to merit and enjoy the good will of the other inhabitants, while every one shall sit in safety under his own vine and fig-tree, and there shall be none to make him afraid.

May the Father of all mercies scatter light and not darkness in our paths, and make us all in our several vocations useful here, and, in his own due time and way, everlastingly happy.

G. Washington

CHAPTER VI

BIBLICAL IMAGERY AND THE REVOLUTION

Even as religious liberty and the separation of church and state became hallmarks of the new Republic, the Bible was helping to shape the new Republic's character, a development which would indirectly affect the course of American Jewish history.

On the eve of the Revolution, the Bible was the most widely known and read literature in the colonies; its influence on colonial culture was preeminent. The Hebrew Scriptures, in particular, enjoyed great popularity, in part, at least, because of the pervasive legacy of New England Puritanism. Certain Puritan Biblical emphases persisted: the stress on Hebrew language; the use of Old Testament names for people and places; the invocation of Biblical practices to legitimate civic affairs. Moreover, Puritan forms of religious rhetoric - jeremiad sermons, Biblical imagery and typological interpretations of the Hebrew Scriptures - continued to reverberate from Yankee pulpits. Given the cultural centrality of the Bible, it is not surprising that both Whigs and Tories sought scriptural legitimacy for their respective political positions.

In sermons, broadsides and pamphlets, patriots drew on Biblical proof-texts from Israelite history to attack the principle of the divine right of kings, to justify revolution against an unresponsive monarch, and to defend republicanism as the preferred form of government. Loyalist Tories mostly looked to the New Testament to justify allegiance to King George III.

By the end of the Revolutionary period, the Puritans' self-identification with the history and heroes of Biblical Israel and their sense of destiny as God's covenantally chosen "new Israel" had broadened to encompass the entire American nation. Many perceived the newly emerging American Republic as heir to the providentially endowed mission of ancient Israel, acting out its millennial role in the world. This outlook, merging national with religious rhetoric, became the overarching motif in America's national self-consciousness and the orienting myth of its civil religion. The roots, metaphors, and theological formulations of this myth were substantially nurtured in the Revolutionary period by American patriotic exegesis of Biblical Israelite history.

Understandably, contemporary American Jews, lineal heirs of Biblical Israel, played no part in the creation of this scripturally-based American national myth. The lines of transmission of the "Biblical heritage" came through Christian rather than Jewish channels; hence, the use of Biblical imagery in the Revolutionary era had little directly to do with American Jewish experience at that time. Still, an examination of the use of Biblical imagery during the Revolution is instructive in at least two respects. It raises the telling but as yet unstudied question as to how American Jews reacted to the identification of their traditional millennial dream with the new Republic at the time of its founding, and it asks how, if at all, they assimilated the new political reality, colored in such familiar religious language, into their own religious orientation.

Of great significance, this chapter provides a useful perspective from which to understand trends of American Jewish apologetics of later years. Both in the nineteenth and twentieth centuries, a good number of Jews pointed to the common Biblical patrimony of Jews and Americans and to the congruity of their Biblically-rooted ideals - freedom, democracy, social justice - to justify their own legitimacy and sense of belongingness as Americans. Moreover, some Jews, especially from within Reform ranks, appropriated for themselves the American national myth of the Republic as the new Zion or Israel and incorporated it into their religious ideology. Thus this American political myth, which had evolved during the Revolutionary era by an integration of Old Testament concepts with national perceptions, later became accepted as an American Jewish religious ideal.

AMERICA'S BIBLICAL HERITAGE: TWO VIEWS

The selections that follow present the views of two scholars representing two different religious traditions on 1) the relationship of the Bible and American identity, and 2) the uses - and occasional misuses - to which Americans have put the Bible. Although they employ different examples, and discuss America's biblical heritage in somewhat different ways, Professors Davis and Noll conclude in remarkably similar fashion. According to Davis, "the biblical heritage became indissoluble from the American tradition." Noll agrees: "the Bible was woven into the warp and woof of American culture . . . its Old Testament narrative had become common coinage for the realm."

AMERICA'S BIBLICAL HERITAGE

Moshe Davis

In the American tradition, the Bible is the source of the common faith, a cohesive force in national aspirations. When the Congress, under the Articles of Confederation, voted in favor of appropriating funds to import twenty thousand copies of the Bible, its members voted, quite literally, to supply a household need. As the most widely read book in America during the colonial era and the nineteenth century, the Bible was the unimpeachable source for both supportive and conflicting opinions in the struggle for political independence and in the antebellum period. In trying as well as glorious times of American history, prophets and idolators, kings and commoners who lived centuries ago in ancient Israel rose to play contemporary roles.

The Fathers of the Republic, for example, did not cite Holy Scriptures in the past tense, but as living, contemporary reality. Their political condition was described as "Egyptian slavery": King George III was Pharaoh; the Atlantic Ocean nothing other than the Red Sea; and Washington and Adams - Moses and Joshua. What could have been a more appropriate seal for the underlying purpose of the Revolution, according to a committee composed of Franklin, Adams, and Jefferson, than the portrayal of the Israelites' exodus from Egypt? In the words of Thomas Jefferson: "Pharaoh sitting in an open chariot, a crown on his head and a sword in his hand passing thro' the divided waters of the Red Sea in pursuit of the Israelites: rays from a pillar of fire in the cloud, expressive of the divine presence, and command, reaching to Moses who stands on the shore and, extending his hand over the sea, causes it to overwhelm Pharaoh." The inscription - a motto by Benjamin Franklin - read: "Rebellion to Tyrants is Obedience to God."

Puritan and Pilgrim identification with biblical thought permeated their political system and gave impetus to a distinctive principle of that system, namely, covenant theology. As Richard B. Morris points out, "This covenant theology (see Genesis 9:8-9, 17:2-4; Exodus 34:10, 28; Psam 106; Jeremiah 31:31) . . . was the keystone to the democratic control of church government. . . . It is government based upon consent of the people, although the Puritan leaders maintained that it must be a government in accord with God's will."

How this ancient civil polity was interpreted in the calls for revolutionary separatism is exemplified in one of the typical "election sermons" - a morality preachment delivered by Samuel Langdon, president of Harvard College, in the Massachusetts Bay Colony, on May 13, 1775:

> The Jewish Government, according to the original constitution which was divinely established, if considered merely in a civil view, was a perfect republic. . . . Every nation, when able and agreed, has a right to set up over themselves any form of government which to them may appear most conducive to their common welfare. The civil polity of Israel is doubtless an excellent general model; allowing for some peculiarities, at least some principal laws and orders of it may be copied to great advantage in more modern establishments.

The Bible was more than a predominating influence on free American institutions. It influenced the individual lives of new Americans, immigrants who came to settle in their "Promised Land." Underlying the events which comprise the history of the United States are the individual sagas of men and women who, each in his or her own way, sought the purpose of their life, the meaning of human existence. To a great extent, this search was centered in the family circle, as its members drew together to study the Bible. Some of the most remarkable treasures may be found in the large family Bibles, in which the records of births, marriages, an deaths were inscribed and which were handed down from parent to child. In these family Bibles we discover the spiritual folklore of America.

Another manifestation of spiritual folklore is the map of America itself. If one's child was to be called by a biblical name, why not one's home, one's town and city? Thus began to appear along America's expanding frontier hundreds of place-names of biblical origin. Numerous places carry such names as Eden, Rehoboth, Sharon, Bethel, Canaan, Hebron, Mamre, Mt. Moriah, Mt. Tabor, Pisgah, Shiloh, Sinai, and Tekoa. Indeed, as one views the "biblical" map of America, one senses how a spiritual folklore was instituted by founders with an intimate knowledge of scriptural sources. Some locations are mentioned only once in the Bible: Elim, Nebraska (Exodus 15:27); Ai, Ohio (Joshua 8:18); Shushan, New York (Book of Esther); Elijah's Zarephath in New Jersey (I Kings 18:8). A Californian in search of gold named his settlement Havilah (Genesis 2:11).

Zion as a place-name reflected the organic relationship between the United States and the Land of Israel. At least fifteen locations are called Zion in almost as many states (Arkansas, Illinois, Iowa, Kentucky, Maryland, Minnesota, Nebraska, New Jersey, North Dakota, Pennsylvania, South Carolina, Utah, and Virginia). Uniquely, Zion City in Illinois was laid out with all its streets bearing biblical names. It was John A. Dowie who, at the end of the nineteenth century, established Zion City, intending it to be governed as a theocracy. For almost four decades the church controlled most of the town's industrial and commercial enterprises. In Shiloh Park, the city was constructed with the church site as its center; branching off it were streets with names taken from the Bible, such as Salem Boulevard, Ebenezer Avenue, Carmel Park, and Jerusalem Boulevard.

A much-favored biblical name dotting the map is Salem. There are no fewer than twenty-seven towns, cities and counties called Salem, and New Jersey has both a city and a county by that name. Thus the founders of these settlements symbolically extended their own "feast of peace" offerings (see Genesis 14:18) to neighboring inhabitants. As is well known, one of America's earliest settlements is Salem, Massachusetts. In 1626-1628, when the Pilgrims received corn from the Indians, they immediately associated the event with the patriarch Abraham and Melchizedek, king of Salem.

Of historical interest is the fact that this particular place-name symbolizes the movement termed progressive pioneering - the transmission of a familial belief from generation to generation. For example, Aaron Street the elder migrated from Salem, New Jersey, to Ohio, where he founded a town by the name of Salem. Together with his son, he moved to Indiana and there founded another town named Salem. The third lap of the journey was by the son to Iowa, where he plotted the Salem in Henry County.

As biblical ideas and images pervaded early American consciousness, the Bible became *The Book* of common knowledge. From it children were taught reading; and as they grew and matured, the indelible pages of the Scriptures, their First Reader, served as their guide, and sometimes even as a determining factor in their vocational choice. One of the most remarkable testimonies of the direct connection between childhood biblical training and vocational purpose is that of the nineteenth-century archaeologist Edward Robinson, whose name today is so closely related to current excavations near the Western Wall. Robinson's Arch is one of the wonders of scholarly ingenuity evidenced for all who come to the reconstructed Temple Mount. In his three-volume *Biblical Researches in Palestine, Mount Sinai and Arabia Petraea*, Robinson writes that his scientific motivation issued from biblical fervor:

As in the case of most of my countrymen, especially in New

England, the scenes of the Bible had made a deep impression upon my mind from the earliest childhood; and afterwards in riper years this feeling had grown into a strong desire to visit in person the places so remarkable in the history of the human race. Indeed in no country of the world, perhaps, is such a feeling more widely diffused than in New England; in no country are the Scriptures better known, or more highly prized. From his earliest years the child is there accustomed not only to read the Bible for himself; but he also reads or listens to it in the morning and evening devotions of the family, in the daily village-school, in the Sunday-school and Bible-class, and in the weekly ministrations of the sanctuary. Hence, as he grows up, the names of Sinai, Jerusalem, Bethlehem, the Promised Land, become associated with his earliest recollections and holiest feelings. . . . With all this, in my own case, there had subsequently become connected a scientific motive. . . .

Thus Americans expressed themselves in personal memory and around the family hearth. In ordeal and triumph, whether in Abraham Lincoln's characterization of the Bible as "the best gift God has given to man" or in Woodrow Wilson's insight that it is the "Magna Charta of the human soul," the biblical heritage became indissoluble from the American tradition.

SOURCE: Moshe Davis (ed.), *With Eyes Toward Zion* (New York, 1977), pp. 4-8. Reprinted by permission of Moshe Davis.

THE IMAGE OF THE UNITED STATES AS A BIBLICAL NATION

Mark A. Noll

On the face of it, it would be hard to imagine a nation more thoroughly biblical than the United States between the American Revolution and the Civil War. The cadences of the Authorized Version informed the writing of the elite and the speech of the humble. One of the ways that Noah Webster, premier wordsmith of the new nation, attempted to reform the country's educational system was to organize early schooling around the reading of his own distinctly American translation of the Bible. For their part, denominational bodies took steps to preserve the integrity of published Bibles, as when Massachusetts Congregationalists and Baptists petitioned Congress in 1790 to regulate the accuracy of printed Bibles. Many Americans also took pains to defend the divine authority of the Bible's message.

This was the period in which Bible societies arose to place a copy of the Scriptures in the hands of every citizen, an effort which even so un-evangelical a figure as Thomas Jefferson supported in 1814 with a $50 contribution. The Monroe County (New York) Bible Society illustrated the thoroughness with which such groups could work by giving a Bible to each of the country's 1200 households that an 1824 census had shown to be without the Scriptures. It was an age when public leaders unabashedly proclaimed their devotion to Scripture. John Adams could call the Bible "the best book in the World." Henry Clay referred to it as "the only book to give us hope in darkness." Daniel Webster asserted that it was "the book of all others for lawyers as well as for divines." And Abraham Lincoln named it "the best gift God has given to man." To be sure, the practice of naming children for biblical characters did begin to decline between the Revolution and the Civil War. Yet the people who influenced public opinion throughout the period were named for biblical figures more often than not. Of the nation's first seventeen Presidents, for example, twelve wore biblical first names. Over 49 percent of the people who published books in 1831 were similarly named.

Once past the obvious fact that the Bible was a ubiquitous presence, however, we discover that the country's biblical character was not simple at all. This is particularly so if we set aside the ways in which Christians used Scripture for private spiritual nourishment and concentrate instead on the public use of the Bible, particularly the ways in which ministers employed Holy Writ to explain the character and destiny of the United States. The problem appears most clearly in sermons preached at times of great national crisis, where even the most superficial sampling leads to a troubling question. Did ministers, preaching from the Bible as public spokesmen, really use Scripture as a primary source for the convictions they expressed? Or did they in fact merely exploit Scripture to sanctify convictions - whether nationalistic, political, social, or racial - which had little to do with biblical themes? The following examples, drawn almost at random from sermons preached at crisis periods in the country's early years, illustrate the seriousness of the difficulty.

In 1773 we find a Connecticut Congregationalist basing a discourse concerning the virtues of home rule and the folly of government by a foreign power on Exodus 1:8 - "Now there arose up a new king over Egypt, which knew not Joseph." A year later a Presbyterian *Sermon on Tea* took Colossians 2:21 for its text - "Touch not; taste not; handle not." During the years of the war itself, a Boston minister inveighed against the "curse" of inflation in a sermon constructed around the story of Achan's deceit at Ai. His text was Joshua 7:13 - "Up, sanctify the people . . . There is an accursed thing in the midst of thee, O Israel: thou canst not stand before thine enemies, until ye take away the accursed thing from among you." When George Washington died in December 1799, the country responded with an outpouring of eulogies, discourses, memorials, and sermons to mark his passing. Of the more than 200 such speeches published in 1800, over 100 were sermons, and of those a full twenty-one used David's lament for Abner in II Samuel 3:38 to mourn the father of his country: "Know ye not that there is a prince and a great man fallen this day in Israel?" During the War of 1812 a New York minister employed the handwriting on the wall at Belshazzar's feast (Daniel 5:27) to weigh the moral character of Great Britain in the balances and find it wanting.

These examples, which could be multiplied virtually without limit, leave the impression that although the Bible may have been the nation's *vade mecum* in times of crisis, it was not in fact the source of the deepest sentiments expressed on those occasions. Rather, ministers seem to have introduced the Bible fairly late into the process of preparing sermonic responses to momentous public events. All too often during the two great wars of the period, a minister's identification with his nation - whether Great Britain or a newly independent United States, whether the Confederacy of the South or the Union of the North - became the fundamental conviction behind the preparation and delivery of sermons. The same pattern was present only slightly less frequently during other crises between the great wars. Public events occurred which seemed to call for sermonic commentary. Ministers prepared and delivered sermons on a text of Scripture. But this text of Scripture became a gateway not for the proclamation of essentially biblical messages but for the minister's social, political, or cultural convictions, which had been securely in place long before he had turned to the Bible.

To come at the public use of Scripture from the inside is to recognize at once that the Bible represented two very different books. It was first a compendium of instruction for faith and practice, a source of universally valid insight about the human condition. At the deaths of Washington and Lincoln, for example, several ministers turned to the wisdom literature of the Old Testament to remind their congregations of verities ordained by God: that the Lord reigned sovereignly over the affairs of men and nations (Psalm 93:1), that a people will long remembers its "righteous" men (Psalm 112:6), or that even godlike rulers must succumb to death with all humanity (Psalm 82:6-7). Used in this way the Bible that spoke to Americans was much the same as that which had spoken to Christians of all times and places.

Much more frequently, however, the Bible was not so much the truth above all truth as it was the story above all stories. On public occasions Scripture appeared regularly as a typical narrative imparting significance to the antitypical events, people, and situations of United States history. That is, ministers preached as if the stories of Scripture were being repeated, or could be repeated, in the unfolding life of the United States. This was as true for white Congregationalists and Presbyterians, decision-makers in American society, as it was for black Baptists and Methodists, who could express their opinions on public affairs only by indirection. Elite whites and slave blacks both looked, for instance, to the Pentateuch as a paradigm for American experience. Whites, at different times and places, saw the Exodus as the model for liberation from Great Britain or from the North; they regarded Moses as the archetype for the United States' own great lawgivers and friends of God. Blacks proclaimed Moses' cry to let his people go with entirely different intentions.

Two convictions were at work in this use of the Bible as the controlling myth for American experience: the belief that Scripture was most useful on public occasions if it was treated as a storehouse of types, and the belief that the United States was an antitype which fulfilled biblical types. These convictions never showed more clearly than when ministers throughout the period invested current events with significance drawn from the history of the ancient Hebrews.

This predisposition to read Scripture typically and to regard the United States as a new Israel naturally led ministers to stress the grand narratives of the Old Testament. Well into the national period, the public Bible of the United States was for all intents the Old Testament. During the Revolution just about the only ministers who preached consistently from the New Testament were pacifists and loyalists, trying - in vain - to overcome the power of Old Testament narratives about setting captive Israel free with straight-forward exposition of New Testament injunctions to honor the king and love one's enemies. When Washington died, only seven of the 120 texts used in published discourses came from the New Testament. And of those seven, four were references to Old Testament characters. A sampling of sermons preached after Lincoln's assassination shows that while the Old Testament was used less frequently than at Washington's death, it still supplied over 70 percent of the texts, and this in spite of the fact that Lincoln died at the end of Holy Week.

The reasons why ministers used the Bible as they did on public occasions in this period are found in a combination of historical influences and of prevailing beliefs about the character of the United States. Historians have frequently noted the importance of the Bible for the English since the Reformation, and the particular importance of the Old Testament for Puritans in Old and New England. They have recognized that although Puritanism had collapsed as a total way of life by the eighteenth century, it continued to exert a powerful influence on the public life of the new United States. They have also described a long English tradition of reading Scripture typologically, a tradition which Cotton Mather brought to a peak in his *Magnalia Christi Americana*. And they have noted the deeply entrenched conviction that the English people were God's elect nation. During the early national period these religious traditions combined with convictions about the United States to create the context for public Bible reading. As many historians have pointed out, heterodox Americans as much as the consistent evangelicals shared convictions about the sacred character and the cosmic destiny of this "first new nation." It is not at all unexpected, then, that the Bible should come to be read in terms dictated by the development of American nationalism.

Once having recognized the lengthy typological tradition and the widely shared beliefs in the special character of the United States, it is not so easy to regard the use of the Bible in the country's early history as simple ideological prostitution or a mere illustration of religious functionalism. It appears, rather, that the Bible was woven into the warp and woof of American culture - that especially its Old Testament images and the flow of its Old Testament narrative had become common coinage for the realm.

SOURCE: Nathan O. Hatch and Mark A. Noll (eds.), *The Bible in America* (New York, 1982), pp. 39-45. Reprinted by permission of Mark A. Noll.

34. Ancient Israel, "A Perfect Republic" - 1775

This attempt to prove the Biblical model of Jewish self-government republican in nature was written to help validate the colonists' republican quest. The sermon from which it comes was preached by Harvard President Samuel Langdon (1722-1797) on May 31, 1775 and is entitled, "Government Corrupted by Vice and Recovered Righteousness."

The Jewish government, according to the original constitution which was divinely established, if considered merely in a civil view, was a perfect republic. The heads of their tribes and elders of their cities were their counsellors and judges. They called the people together in more general or particular assemblies, - took their opinions, gave advice, and managed the public affairs according to the general voice. Counsellors and judges comprehend all the powers of that government; for there was no such thing as legislative authority belonging to it, - their complete code of laws being given immediately from God by the hand of Moses. And let them who cry up the divine right of kings consider that the only form of government which had a proper claim to a divine establishment was so far from including the idea of a king, that it was a high crime for Israel to ask to be in this respect like other nations; and when they were gratified, it was rather as a just punishment of their folly, that they might feel the burdens of court pageantry, of which they were warned by a very striking description, than as a divine recommendation of kingly authority.

35. *"Worse Than Egyptian Darkness" - 1775*

This letter filled with Biblical allusions, was sent by an unidentified man to his correspondent in London and was published in the London Evening Post, *November 23-25, 1775. One of the most significant sources of news on the feelings and conditions in America available to the English were personal letters written from colonists to friends and relatives in England. Often these letters found their way into the columns of the English press, where they appeared anonymously without signature or with only the initials signed.*

Surely the people at large of Great Britain, are involved in worse than Egyptian darkness, while their rulers are madly rushing, like Pharaoh and his host, through a sea of blood, on their utter destruction. Our people commiserate the situation of the British soldiery; but if foreign mercenaries should come over, the most cowardly of the Americans will be inspired with courage, and they will not meet with like pity; we are well prepared to meet *any* force that can be sent against us. The Americans in general are as well disciplined as Regulars, and have plenty of ammunition; above all, Providence smiles on our righteous cause, and our Country. The earth this year has been laden with riches; never were such great crops taken from it of every kind, so that there can be no danger of starving; and our troops have had such success in every enterprize, that the hand of Heaven seems visibly on our side: even the bloody affair at Bunker's Hill was such a galling stroke to the Regulars, that a few more victories of a similar kind would utterly destroy them. The battle at the islands near Boston was a very great action, as General Gage lost above 300 men, without the loss on our side of any more than one single American. In short, when I survey ever step heretofore taken, I cannot but conclude, in the words of an old fashioned book, seldom consulted by kings or their ministers: "The kinds of the earth stand up, and their rulers take council together; but He, by whom kings reign, shall laugh them to scorn, even the Holy one shall have them in derision." Sooner or later he will vindicate his own divine prerogative by the overthrow of tyrants and of tyranny.

36. A Proposed Seal for the United States - 1776

Pictured here is an artist's reconstruction of a proposed seal for the United States submitted by a committee of Benjamin Franklin, John Adams, and Thomas Jefferson, to the Continental Congress at its request. One side of the seal depicts the Israelites and Moses, his arms outstretched and rays of light from a pillar of fire beaming on his face, standing on the shore while Pharaoh and his army drown in the Red Sea; the accompanying phrase reads "Rebellion to tyrants is obedience to God." This highlights the favored and prevalent Biblical metaphor used by revolutionaries to describe their struggle - the patriots as latter day Israelites fighting the tyranny of those contemporary Egyptians, the British. The obverse side of the seal, usually ignored by later American Jewish historians, shows "Hengist and Horsa, the Saxon chiefs." The committee felt they represented the other source of American descent "whose political principles and form of government we have assumed."

REVERSE.

OBVERSE.

37. "The King Hearkened Not Unto the People:
For the Cause Was From the Lord" - 1777

    The title and excerpt from this sermon, preached by William Gordon (1728-1807), Pastor of the Third Church in Roxbury on July 4, 1777, in the Massachusetts House of Representatives, illustrate the kind of typological Biblical analysis which sought to link episodes in Jewish Biblical history with events in contemporary America. In this instance, the Jews' rebellion against the tyranny of King Solomon's son Rehoboam, resulting in a permanent split in the Jewish nation, serves as prototype and justification for the American revolt against George III. To Gordon and his audience, the scriptural judgment rendered in I Kings 12:15, "wherefore the king hearkened not unto the people: for the cause was from the Lord," resonated with contemporary meaning.

The Separation of the Jewish
Tribes, After The Death Of
Solomon, Accounted For,
And Applied To The
Present Day,

In A

SERMON

Preached Before the

GENERAL COURT,

On Friday, July the 4th, 1777.

Being

The Anniversary of the Declaration
of
Independency.

BY WILLIAM GORDON.
Pastor of the Third Church in Roxbury.

. . . I have considered the revolution that commenced at the death of Solomon, and the progress of that separation from the house of David, that the ten tribes were drove into, by the insulting and tyrannical conduct of Rehoboam - an event of that nature and so circumstanced, that can be accounted for only upon the principle assigned by the sacred historian - *the king hearkened not unto the people, for the cause was from the Lord.* And it is upon that principle alone that we can rationally account for the separation that hath taken place, between the united States of America and Great Britain.

You must have applied already much of the discourse; for *we* have not been alluding to things done in secret; and you cannot be dwellers in the Massachusetts, and be strangers to them. This continent complained of real grievances, and *humbly petitioned.* Whatever individuals of uncommon penetration might wish, from foreseeing what would necessarily exist sooner or later; the bulk of the people in every *State, not this excepted,* the body of the delegates, would have been satisfied, would have rejoiced, would have been happy, had their requests been complied with. No set of delegates could have insisted upon more without breaking the union of the colonies. Instead of being heard and relieved, the yoke was increased by frest acts of cruelty, and new burdens laid upon the continent. Our first grievances were spoken of, as if not real; and as tho' we complained without cause, it was determined that we should have cause for complaining. We had not been accustomed to a state of slavery; therefore could not brook such treatment without resenting it.

38. Nicholas Street's Jeremiad - 1777

This excerpt from a jeremiad preached by Rev. Nicholas Street in his East Haven, Connecticut church in April, 1777 draws parallels between the experience of the Israelites and the colonists, but does so for the purpose of promoting internal introspection and reform among the colonists. The terrible injustices inflicted by the Pharaoh Britain should not blind colonial inhabitants to their own sins, he says; only after these sins are repudiated will the colonists enter the promised land of political independence.

The American States Acting
Over the Part of The Children
Of Israel In The Wilderness
And Thereby Impeding Their
Entrance Into Canaan's Rest

Deuteronomy viii.2.   *"And thou shalt remember all the way which the Lord thy GOD led thee these forty years in the wilderness, to humble thee, and to prove thee, to know what was in thine heart, whether thou wouldest keep his commandments or no."*

The history of the children of Israel in Egypt, their sufferings and oppression under the tyrant Pharaoh, their remarkable deliverance by the hand of Moses out of that state of bondage and oppression, and their trials and murmurings in the wilderness, is well known by those who have been conversant with their bibles, and have attended to those important lessons contained in the five Books of Moses. But why God thus dealth with that people, perhaps has not been duly attended to by those that have made conscience of reading the sacred story. But the text tells us, that it was to humble them, and to prove them, that they might know what was in their hearts, and whether they would keep his commandments, or no. All the events which befel them in the way; the miraculous protections, deliverances, provisions and instructions which God gave them, and withal, the frequent and severe punishments which were inflicted for their disobedience, was to discover to themselves and others, all that infidelity, inconstancy, hypocrisy, apostacy, rebellion and perverseness which lay hid in their hearts; the discovery of which was of singular use both to them, and to the church of God in all succeeding ages. For as Watts has it,

There, as in a glass our hearts may see,
How fickle and how false they be.

God, by them, designed to let after generations know what was in their hearts. But it is not generally known and believed till it comes to the trial; and then it is found that we are prone to act over the same stupid vile part that the children of Israel did in the wilderness, under the most instructive and speaking providences that ever obtained in the world. . . .

We in this land are, as it were, led out of Egypt by the hand of Moses. And now we are in the wilderness, i.e. in a state of trouble and difficulty, Egyptians pursuing us, to overtake us and reduce us. There is the Red Sea before us, I speak metaphorically, a sea of blood in your prospect before you, perhaps. And when you apprehend this in your imaginations, are you not ready to murmur against Moses and Aaron that led you out of Egypt, and to say with the people of Israel, "It had been better for us to serve the Egyptians, than that we should die in the wilderness." Exod. 14.12. And tho' God has been pleased to work marvellously for us at times as he did for them; yet if any new difficulty arises, and if things don't go on so prosperously as at other times, how soon does our faith fail us, and we begin to murmur against Moses and Aaron, and wish ourselves back again in Egypt, where we had some comforts of life, which we are now deprived of? not considering that we chose our leaders, and that in obtaining any deliverance there are great troubles and difficulties generally attending it; neither considering that our ill successes are owing to the sins of the people, as was the case of the people of Israel in the wilderness. We find them ten times as ready to find fault with their leaders, and to ascribe their misfortunes to them, as to recoil in upon themselves, and to say, What have we done? tho' it was owing entirely to them that they were not delivered. And thus we in this land are murmuring and complaining of our difficulties and ill successes at times, thinking our leaders to blame, and the like, not considering at the same time that we are practising those vices that a natural tendency to destroy us, besides the just judgments of Heaven which they tend to draw down upon us as a people. . . . And when we are favoured with a little success, we are apt to be elated in our minds like the children of Israel after the overthrow of the Egyptians in the red sea, and then with them to rejoice, and to encourage ourselves in the cause in which we are engaged; then we can trust, as we imagine, in God, and hope for his salvation and deliverance. But let the scale turn a little against us, our confidence begins to fail, and we grow distrustful of God and his providence, and begin to murmur and repine.

39. America as the New Israel - 1783

The election day sermon by Ezra Stiles (1727-1795) from which this selection is taken was delivered on May 8, 1783. President of Yale University and an outstanding Hebraist whose interests in Jewish and Hebrew literature ranged broadly, Stiles was at once both an admirer of the Israelites and their faith and a Christian triumphalist who hoped for the ultimate conversion of the Jews. This selection contains one of the clearest expressions identifying America as the new Israel, that nation to which Biblical prophecies had been pointing and in which they were now being fulfilled.

And to make thee high above all nations which he hath made, in praise, and in name, and in honor; and that thou mayest be an holy people unto the Lord thy God. - Deut. xxvi.10.

Taught by the omniscient Deity, Moses foresaw and predicted the capital events relative to Israel, through the successive changes of depression and glory, until their final elevation to the first dignity and eminence among the empires of the world. These events have been so ordered as to become a display of retribution and sovereignty; for, while the good and evil hitherto felt by this people have been dispensed in the way of exact national retribution, their ultimate glory and honor will be of the divine sovereignty, with a "Not for your sakes do I this, saith the Lord, be it known unto you, but for mine holy name's sake."

However it may be doubted whether political communities are rewarded and punished in this world only, and whether the prosperity and decline of other empires have corresponded with their moral state as to virtue and vice, yet the history of the Hebrew theocracy shows that the secular welfare of God's ancient people depended upon their virtue, their religion, their observance of that holy covenant which Israel entered into with God on the plains at the foot of Nebo, on the other side Jordan. Here Moses, the man of God, assembled three million of people, - the number of the United States, - recapitulated and gave them a second publication of the sacred jural institute, delivered thirty-eight years before, with the most awful solemnity, at Mount Sinai. A law dictated with sovereign authority by the Most High to a people, to a world, a universe, becomes of invincible force and obligation without any reference to the consent of the governed. It is obligatory for three reasons, viz., its original justice and unerring equity, the omnipotent Authority by which it is enforced, and the sanctions of rewards and punishments. But in the case of Israel he condescended to a mutual covenant, and by the hand of Moses led his people to avouch the Lord Jehovah to be their God, and in the most public and explicit manner voluntarily to engage and covenant with God to keep and obey his law. Thereupon this great prophet, whom God had raised up for so solemn a transaction, declared in the name of the Lord that the Most High avouched, acknowledged, and took them for a peculiar people to himself; promising to be their God and Protector, and upon their obedience to make them prosperous and happy. He foresaw, indeed, their rejection of God, and predicted the judicial chastisement of apostasy - a chastisement involving the righteous with the wicked. But, as well to comfort and support the righteous in every age, and under every calamity, as to make his power known among all nations, God determined that a remnant should be saved. Whence Moses and the prophets, by divine direction, interspersed their writings with promises that when the ends of God's moral government should be answered in a series of national punishments, inflicted for a succession of ages, he would, by his irresistible power and sovereign grace subdue the hearts of his people to a free, willing, joyful obedience; turn their captivity; recover and gather them "from all the nations whither the Lord had scattered them in his fierce anger; bring them into the land which their fathers possessed; and multiply them above their fathers, and rejoice over them for good, as he rejoiced over their fathers." Then the words of Moses, hitherto accomplished but in part, will be literally fulfilled, when this branch of the posterity of Abraham shall be nationally collected, and become a very distinguished and glorious people, under the great Messiah, the Prince of Peace. He will then "make them high above all nations which he hath made, in praise, and in name, and in honor, and they shall become a holy people unto the Lord their God."

I shall enlarge no further upon the primary sense and literal accomplishment of this and numerous other prophecies respecting both Jews and Gentiles in the latter-day glory of the church; for I have assumed the text only as introductory to a discourse upon the political welfare of God's American Israel, and as allusively prophetic of the future prosperity and splendor of the United States.

40."Sound the Great Horn For Our Freedom": A Shearith Israel Prayer - 1784

This prayer is one of the few sources available in which one can see how Jews applied Biblical imagery to the contemporary American situation. Composed by Rabbi Hendla Jochanan van Oettingen and delivered by Jacob R. Cohen in New York's Shearith Israel in 1784, it acknowledges that the spirit of the Biblical God rested on American leaders such as Washington and expresses the hope that these men will deal kindly with Israel. With sermonic flourish, Cohen prays that the freedom gained by the thirteen states will foreshadow the fulfillment of the traditional Jewish hope of messianic restoration to Zion. This sentiment is a far cry, of course, from identification of the new Republic with the long-awaited millennium.

We (turn) towards God and towards God are our eyes. Blessed be the Lord who has dealt kindly with us, in His mercy and great kindness He has dealt magnanimously with us. By the breath of His mouth He has created heaven and earth and the world and those who dwell thereon. He gives light to the earth and its inhabitants. He has created all created things, and every existing thing He has produced, what exists created from the non-existent.

King eternal, to Him is Kingship, and He causes monarchs to reign. He it is who implanted peace in the heart of kings so that they may return the sword to its sheath. The Lord has said peace to those afar and to those near. We will praise the Lord in congregation for His kindnesses which He has benevolently bestowed upon us. We cried unto the Lord from our straits and from our troubles He brought us forth. And for us, a weak people, inhabiting the land, He in His goodness prospered our warfare. Thou hast restored us our inheritance from the hands of aliens and strangers and given us back the joy of our heart.

And now, King, exalted beyond all height, we have come to pour out our soul before Thee. Hear the prayer of Thy first-born son, Thy peculiar people, who trust in Thy thirteen attributes of mercy, that they return not empty from before Thee, faithful sons of faithful believers in the thirteen principles of Thy Law.

As Thou didst give of Thy glory to David, son of Jesse, and to Solomon his son Thou didst give wisdom greater than that of all men, so mayst Thou grant intelligence, wisdom, and knowledge to our lords, the rulers of these thirteen states, to judge the people, yea also to the commanding general, GOVERNOR CLINTON, together with their counsellors, advisers, (officers and deputies) each ruling in his sphere, each man by his standard, each upon whose shoulder Thou hast set dominion. May he be upheld and his honor be high. May he be as the fresh olive tree, and blossom as the lily of the valley, as the rose of

Sharon, and may he be as the tree planted by springs of water, whose fruit cometh forth in its due season and its leaf withereth not. And in whatsoever he doeth may he prosper.

And as in their great kindness they will deal well with us, and we shall dwell in quietness and peace in their shadow, so mayst Thou reward them according to their desert. Give to them the desires of their heart, so that they may deal well with us unceasingly. Cause us to find favor and grace in their eyes that they may set us a seal upon their heart. O that this may be Thy will and let us say Amen.

As Thou didst give strength to Samson, the son of Manoah that he rent a young lion in his might, so mayst Thou strengthen and support the saving shield of our lord and commanding general GEORGE WASHINGTON, the appointed chief of the war on sea and on land and throughout the country with all his forces infantry and cavalry. In Thine own time Thou wilt subdue the people beneath his feet until they turn their back to him and not their face; may they fall and rise up no more, and may he pursue his enemies, and overtaking them, not return until they are destroyed. O Lord save us now! O Lord prosper us now! O how goodly, how beautiful might it be wouldst Thou confirm the peace that Thou hast planted on the hearts of kings and rulers that they should beat their swords into plowshares, their spears into pruning forks, that nation should not lift up sword against nation nor should they any more learn war; that Thou wouldst establish over us the word that is written: "And I will set peace in the land and you shall dwell with none to make you afraid. Great is the peace to those who love Thy teaching, for them is no stumbling block. May peace be in thy rampart, prosperity in thy palaces." Set mercy in their heart that they may deal kindly with us and with all Israel through the merit of the love of the patriarchs, as it is written: "And I shall remember my convenant with Jacob, also my covenant with Isaac, yea also my covenant with Abraham and the land shall I remember." O that this may be Thy will and let us say Amen.

As Thou hast granted to these thirteen states of America everlasting freedom, so mayst Thou bring us forth once again from bondage into freedom, and mayst Thou sound the great horn for our freedom as it is said: "And it shall be on that day, the great horn shall be blown and the wanderers in the land of Assyria and the dispersed in the land of Egypt shall come and bow down to the Lord on the holy mount in Jerusalem." May they be awakened from the dust to praise God: Hasten our deliverance at the day of retribution for Thou art our Redeemer. Then shall we sing a new song to the Lord, God of Israel, and there we shall serve Him with reverence as in the former days of old. May He show us wonders as in days of old, and may He the Holy One, blessed be He, restore the Presence to Zion and the order of service to Jerusalem. And may we be granted to gaze on the beauty of the Lord and to behold His sanctuary. May He send us the priest of righteousness who will lead us upright to our land. May the beauty of the

Lord be upon us, and may the redeemer come speedily to Zion in our days. O that this may be Thy will and let us say Amen.

GUIDE TO AVAILABLE RESOURCES AND MATERIALS
on
JEWS AND THE FOUNDING OF THE REPUBLIC

Filmstrips

1. "Jewish National Fund Salutes the Bicentennial"

> The filmstrip includes original art work depicting Jewish part-
> icipation in the American Revolution. Slides (frames) of the
> Bicentennial Park in Israel trace the similarities between the
> achievement of independence in the United States and Israel.
> 55 frames   UAHC*

2. "Jews in America"

> A two-part program with archival drawing, documents, and
> photographs. A depiction of Jewish life in America from Colonial
> times.
> Color (with cassette)   BB

Slides and Tapes

1. "Haym Salomon: A Gentleman of Precision and Integrity"

> The life and times of Haym Salomon is reviewed including a
> historiography of early American Jewry.
> 20 minutes   JMS

2. "The American Jew"

> Using archival materials, this program tells the story of the Jew
> in America since 1654.
> Color (with cassette)   AJHS

Films (16 mm)

1. "Degree of Freedom"

> Thomas Jefferson's fight for religious freedom for all citizens.
> 30 minutes - black and white   NAAJS
>   JMS

---

*Key to Abbreviations of Distributors on Page 131.

2. "A Heritage of Freedom"

   A story of the earliest Jewish settlers in America.
   25 minutes - black and white   JMS

3. "The Red Box"

   An episode in the life of Gershom Seixas regarding his fight
   for freedom of religious beliefs.
   30 minutes - black and white   NAAJS

4. "Rendezvous with Freedom"

   This ABC documentary on the course of American Jewish
   history has an especially fine segment about early
   colonial days.
   56 minutes - color
   (also 32 minute version)   JMS

5. "Trapdoor"

   The story of the Newport synagogue and how the Jewish
   colonists built a trapdoor in the pulpit for escape in
   case of attack.
   25 minutes - black and white   JMS

6. "Heritage: Civilization and the Jews"
   Program Seven: "Golden Land"

   This program (seventh of nine shown on PBS) has an interesting
   and informative section concerning the Colonial Jew.
   color - with study guide   FI

Key to the Abbreviations of Distributors:

   JMS -   Jewish Media Service
                National Jewish Welfare Board
                15 East 26th Street
                New York, NY 10010

   NAAJS -   National Academy of Adult Jewish Studies
                155 Fifth Avenue
                New York, NY 10010

   UAHC -   Union of American Hebrew Congregations
                838 Fifth Avenue
                New York, NY 10021

BB -   B'nai B'rith
              315 Lexington Avenue
              New York, NY 10016

AJHS -   American Jewish Historical Society
              2 Thornton Road
              Waltham, MA 02154

FI -   Films, Inc.
              1213 Wilmette Avenue
              Suite #202
              Wilmette, IL 60091

Documents

The American Jewish Historical Society, 2 Thornton Road, Waltham, MA 02154, (617) 891-8110, and the American Jewish Archives, 3101 Clifton Avenue, Cincinnati, OH 45220, (513) 221-1875 contain numerous documents relating to "Jews and the Founding of the Republic." They will usually send Xerox copies. For other repositories which may contain documentary materials, see the latest edition of *The Directory of Historical Societies and Agencies in the United States and Canada*, published by the American Association for State and Local History (Nashville, Tennessee).

Novels

The following novels depict the life of Jews in the New Nation:

1. Howard Fast, *The Proud and the Free* (Boston: 1950)
       Depicts anti-Semitism in a Pennsylvania regiment.

2. Robert Gessner, *Treason* (New York: 1944)
       Haym Salomon is portrayed as part of this fictionalized account of Benedict Arnold's treachery.

3. Louis Zara, *This Land is Ours* (Boston: 1940)
       Jews feature as part of this panoramic novel covering the period from the Revolution to the Civil War.

Posters

The American Jewish Archives, 3101 Clifton Avenue, Cincinnati, Ohio 45220 has a series of posters available free for the asking.

1. "A Rabbi in Colonial Newport"
       Haim Isaac Carigal, 1773

2. "Isaac Franks"
   He fought with Washington, was captured by British in 1776, later escaped.

3. "Abigail Minis"
   She left Savannah for South Carolina rather than live under British rule.

4. "Philip Minis - Levi Sheftall"
   These men guided the patriot forces to Savannah, when they recaptured the city in 1779.

5. "Subversion in British Held New York"
   Haym Salomon acted as a secret agent in New York.

6. "Mordecai Sheftall"
   He was captured by British in Savannah, 1778.

7. "Sheftall Sheftall"
   He brought money and food to the relief of General Moultrie and his soldiers who had been captured by the British.

8. "Levy Solomons"
   He aided the American invaders of Canada, 1775.

Photographs

Hannah R. London has written two books that portray Jews who lived during America's early years: *Portraits of Jews by Gilbert Stuart and Other Early American Artists* (Rutland, VT: 1969); and *Miniatures and Silhouettes of Early American Jews* (Rutland, VT: 1970).

The American Jewish Archives has an extensive picture collection, some examples from which are found in this volume. See also *An Index to the Picture Collection of the American Jewish Archives* (Cincinnati, OH: 1977). Other picture collections may be found at the American Jewish Historical Society and New York Public Library.

United States Postage Stamps

1. 1975 "Haym Salomon" "Contributors to the Cause"   [$.10]

2. 1982 "Touro Synagogue (Newport)" - "National Landmark"   [$.20]

Landmarks

American Jewish Landmarks, Vols. I-III, by Bernard Postal and Lionel Koppman (New York, NY: 1977, 1984) contain a very extensive listing of landmarks arranged geographically with a fine index. Some relate to Jewish participants in the forging of the Republic, for example:

1. Isaac Franks House - used by George Washington as the Executive
   Mansion in Philadelphia, PA

2. A statue of "George Washington, Robert Morris, Haym Salomon"
   located on Wacker Drive, Chicago, IL

3. A statue of "Haym Salomon" located in MacArthur Park,
   Los Angeles, CA

American Bicentennial Carton

The Union of American Hebrew Congregations, 838 Fifth Avenue,
New York, NY 10021, produced these materials concerning Jewish
participation in the American Revolution.

Of particular interest may be:

1. A large picture of Jacob Hart who donated money to General
   Lafayette for food and clothing for the troops.

2. A picture of the Isaac Franks House in Philadelphia.

3. A large picture of Jonas Phillips.

BIBLIOGRAPHY

I. TEXTBOOKS

*Feingold, Henry L. *Zion in America: The Jewish Experience from Colonial Times to the Present.* New York: Hippocrene Books, 1974.

> Chapters 2-3 contain information and background on Jews and the Founding of the Republic.

Karp, Abraham J. *Haven and Home: A History of the Jews in America.* New York: Schocken, 1985.

> Chapters 1-2 cover early America and reprint several key documents.

*Learsi, Rufus [Israel Goldberg]. *The Jews in America: A History.* New York: Ktav, 1972.

> Chapter 3 surveys "Revolution and Emancipation."

II. DOCUMENTS

Friedenwald, Herbert. "Jews Mentioned in the Journal of the Continental Congress," in *The Jewish Experience in America,* I, edited by Abraham J. Karp. Waltham: American Jewish Historical Society, 1969, pp. 319-343.

> Trace the various correspondences and business dealings between Jews and the Congress as reflected in the *Journal.* Reprinted from the *Publications of the American Jewish Historical Society,* I (1893).

Marcus, Jacob Rader (ed.). *American Jewry. Documents. Eighteenth Century.* Cincinnati: Hebrew Union College Press, 1959 [reprinted, New York: Ktav, 1976].

> A remarkable collection of 196 documents dealing with all facets of eighteenth century life, with introductions and notes. Many of the documents date to the period of the founding of the republic.

*Marcus Jacob Rader (ed.). *Jews and the American Revolution: A Bicentennial Documentary.* Cincinnati: American Jewish Archives, 1975.

> An outstanding collection of sources illuminating in its breadth and diversity the full scope of the Jewish experience in Revolutionary America. Contains an insightful introductory essay by the author as well as annotated notes for each document. Originally published as a special issue in volume 27 of *American Jewish Archives* (November 1975).

*Schappes, Morris U. (ed.). *A Documentary History of the Jews in the United States 1654-1875.* New York: Schocken Books, 1971.

> About twenty of the documents in this 766 page volume deal with the founding of the republic. Schappes' choice of documents is

---

*paperback edition available

excellent and his introductions and notes are often highly illuminating.

III. SURVEYS: JEWS AND THE FOUNDING OF THE REPUBLIC

Marcus, Jacob R. *The Colonial American Jew 1492-1776.* Detroit: Wayne State University Press, 1970.

> The last five chapters of this magisterial work deal with Jews and the Revolution in elaborate detail, with extensive footnotes.

Morris, Richard B. "The Jews, Minorities, and Dissent in the American Revolution." *Migration and Settlement: Proceedings of the Anglo-American Jewish Historical Conference.* London: 1971, pp. 146-164.

> A very insightful overview highlighting the various Jewish postures and activities during the Revolutionary War. A somewhat briefer version of this article, without notes, is to be found in Gladys Rosen (ed.), *Jewish Life in America: Historical Perspectives,* New York: Ktav, 1978, pp. 8-27.

Rezneck, Samuel. *Unrecognized Patriots: The Jews in the American Revolution.* Westport, CT: Greenwood Press, 1975.

> A comprehensive survey of the period with notes and bibliography. The best one-volume work in the field.

Sarna, Jonathan D. "The Impact of the American Revolution on American Jews," *Modern Judaism,* I (September 1981), pp. 149-160.

> An analysis of how the American Revolution affected the social, economic, political and religious condition of American Jewry; extensively documented.

IV. SPECIAL STUDIES

1. Jews and the American Revolution

Chyet, Stanley F. *Lopez of Newport: Colonial American Merchant Prince.* Detroit: Wayne State University Press, 1970.

> Aaron Lopez (1731-1782) was one of the leading Jews of his day. He was involved in the struggle for independence and was deeply affected by it.

Grinstein, Hyman B. *The Rise of the Jewish Community of New York, 1654-1860.* Philadelphia: Jewish Publication Society, 1945.

> Deals with New York Jews and the Revolution under various headings; see index "American Revolution."

Gutstein, Morris A. *The Story of the Jews of Newport.* New York: Bloch Publishing Company, 1936.

> Details the story of Newport Jews in the American Revolution.

Kaganoff, Nathan M. "The Business Career of Haym Salomon as Reflected in His Newspaper Advertisements," *American Jewish*

Historical Quarterly, 66 (September 1976), pp. 35-49.

A fresh perspective on Salomon, the best-known Jew of the Revolutionary era, indicating his acute awareness of advertising's potential benefit to business.

Marcus, Jacob R. *The Handsome Young Priest in the Black Gown: The Personal World of Gershom Seixas.* Cincinnati: American Jewish Archives, 1970 [originally published in *Hebrew Union College Annual*, vols. 40-41 (1969-1970)].

Gershom Seixas (1746-1816) was minister of Congregation Shearith Israel in New York at the time of the Revolution. He fled first to Stratford and then to Philadelphia.

Reznikoff, Charles and Engelman, Uriah Z. *The Jews of Charleston.* Philadelphia: Jewish Publication Society, 1950.

Contains sections describing the role of Charleston Jews in the Revolution and the impact of independence on the Jewish community's development.

Roth, Cecil. "Some Jewish Loyalists in the War of American Independence," *The Jewish Experience in America*, I, edited by Abraham J. Karp. Waltham: American Jewish Historical Society, 1969, pp. 292-318.

A description of some of the major Jewish figures and their families who embraced the Tory cause. Reprinted from the *Publications of the American Jewish Historical Society*, 38 (1948).

Wolf, Edwin 2nd and Whiteman, Maxwell. *The History of the Jews of Philadelphia from Colonial Times to the Age of Jackson.* Philadelphia: Jewish Publication Society, 1956, 1975.

Several chapters examine the role of Philadelphia Jews in the founding of the republic, and America's subsequent impact on the Jewish community.

2. Biblical Imagery and the Revolution

The American Republic and Ancient Israel. New York: Arno Press, 1977.

Reprints three very important sermons by prominent New England clergymen illustrating typological analysis of the Biblical text, and the application of Bible lessons to contemporary times.

*Bercovitch, Sacvan. *The American Jeremiad.* Madison: University of Wisconsin Press, 1978.

An incisive analysis of the Puritan use of the jeremiad sermon and how its rhetoric became adapted by later generations to fashion such pivotal American myths as "the new chosen people," "American Israel" and "manifest destiny."

Berens, John F. *Providence and Patriotism in Early America, 1640-1815.* Charlottesville: University Press of Virginia, 1978.

This excellent work, with its exhaustive evaluation of sermons during the Revolutionary period, traces the evolution of civil millennialism and the progression of providential thought in American life.

Davis, Moshe. "The Holy Land Idea in American Spiritual History," in *With Eyes Toward Zion*, Moshe Davis (ed.). New York: Arno Press, 1977, pp. 3-33.

A concise, penetrating evaluation of the impact of the Biblical heritage and the idea of the Holy Land in American life.

Hatch, Nathan O. *The Sacred Cause of Liberty: Republican Thought and Millennialism in Revolutionary New England*. New Haven: Yale University Press, 1977.

A fine analysis of the convergence of religious, millennial and political republican thought in this time period.

Hay, Robert P. "George Washington: American Moses," *American Quarterly*, 21 (1969), pp. 780-791.

Based on an analysis of the great number of funeral orations on Washington upon his death, this article demonstrates clearly how the American hero became almost the reincarnation of the Biblical Moses in American consciousness.

Katsh, Abraham I. *The Biblical Heritage of American Democracy*. New York: Ktav, 1977.

A descriptive, somewhat filiopietistic overview of the impact of the Bible and Hebraic spirit on the American people, especially on the Puritans. Excellent illustrations, and pertinent historical sidelights in appendices.

Leighly, John. "Biblical Place-Names in the United States," *Names*, 27 (1979), pp. 46-59.

A description of Biblical place-names in the United States and their distribution, indicating among other things, that with the exceptions of Bethany, Bethlehem, Corinth and Philadelphia, all biblical names in colonial times came from the Hebrew Bible.

Meyer, Isidore S. "The Book of Esther: American Midrash," *Hebrew Studies*, 17 (1976), pp. 49-68.

An interesting historical account of the typological analysis of the Biblical Book of Esther, with its villains of Haman and Ahasuerus and its heroes of Mordecai and Esther, and its contemporary applications by supporters of various American causes from 1763 to the eve of the Revolution.

Neuman, Abraham A. "Relation of the Hebrew Scriptures to American Institutions," *Landmarks and Goals*, Philadelphia: Dropsie College, 1953, pp. 255-275.

A descriptive somewhat filiopietistic overview.

*Noll, Mark A. "The Image of the United States as a Biblical Nation, 1776-1865," *The Bible in America: Essays in Cultural History*, ed. Nathan O. Hatch and Mark A. Noll. New York: Oxford University Press, 1982, pp. 39-58.

> A well-documented interpretive essay, indicating how the Hebrew Bible was used as prototype for the destiny and character of American history, especially in moments of crisis.

Straus, Oscar S. *The Origin of Republican Form of Government in the United States of America*. New York: 1885, 1901.

> An outstanding example of filiopietistic history which argues that the political model for American republicanism was the republican Hebrew Commonwealth from the time of the Exodus until King Saul.

3. The New Nation and the Jews

Baron, Salo W. "The Emancipation Movement and American Jewry," *Steeled by Adversity: Essays and Addresses on American Jewish Life*, edited by Jeannette Meisel Baron. Philadelphia: Jewish Publication Society, 1971.

> An examination of American independence in the broad context of worldwide Jewish emancipation.

Borden, Morton. *Jews, Turks and Infidels*. Chapel Hill, NC: University of North Carolina Press, 1984.

> A full length study of the Jewish struggle for religious equality in America.

Chyet, Stanley F. "The Political Rights of the Jews in the United States: 1776-1840," *American Jewish Archives*, 10 (1958), pp. 14-75.

> An exhaustive state-by-state analysis.

Eitches, Edward. "Maryland's Jew Bill," *American Jewish Historical Quarterly*, 60 (March 1971), pp. 258-279.

> A new analysis of the controversy over the bill to grant Jews equality in Maryland, which places the question in the context of state politics; heavily documented.

Handlin, Oscar and Mary. "The Acquisition of Political and Social Rights by the Jews in the United States," *American Jewish Year Book*, 56 (1955), pp. 43-98.

> One section of this broad survey deals with "the consequences of independence."

*Handy, Robert T. *The American Revolution and Religious Freedom*. The Sol Feinstone Lecture for 1979. New York: Jewish Theological Seminary, 1979.

> Discusses six major factors which helped to bring about disestablishment and religious freedom in the Revolutionary era.

Jews, Judaism and the American Constitution. Pamphlet Series of the American Jewish Archives, No. III. Cincinnati: American Jewish Archives, 1982.

> Contains two wide-ranging and amply documented essays: "The Confluence of Torah and Constitution," by Milton R. Konvitz, and "Jews and Jewry in American Constitutional History," by Leo Pfeffer.

Stokes, Anson Phelps. *Church and State in the United States.* 3 vols. New York: Harper and Row, 1954.

> This magisterial, heavily documented study remains the basic work in the field. A one-volume revised edition, by Leo Pfeffer, was published in 1964.

SOURCES

Document 1. Jacob R. Marcus (ed.) *Jews and the American Revolution: A Bicentennial Documentary* (Cincinnati, 1975), pp. 117-118.

Document 2. *Publications of the American Jewish Historical Society,* 27 (1920), pp. 31-32.

Document 3. Marcus, *Jews and the American Revolution,* p. 121.

Document 4. Marcus, *Jews and the American Revolution,* p. 121.

Document 5. Lee M. Friedman, *Jewish Pioneers and Patriots* (Philadelphia, 1942), p. 347.

Document 6. Marcus, *Jews and the American Revolution,* p. 135.

Document 7. Marcus, *Jews and the American Revolution,* pp. 128-129.

Document 8. *Publications of the American Jewish Historical Society,* 23 (1915), p. 177.

Document 9. Marcus, *Jews and the American Revolution,* pp. 151-154.

Document 10. Marcus, *Jews and the American Revolution,* pp. 149-150.

Document 11. Morris U. Schappes (ed.), *A Documentary History of the Jews in the United States 1654-1875* (New York, 1950), pp. 58-61.

Document 12. Jacob R. Marcus (ed.), *American Jewry. Documents. Eighteenth Century* (Cincinnati, 1959), pp. 427-428.

Document 13. Marcus, *Jews and the American Revolution,* pp. 174-175.

Document 14. Marcus, *Jews and the American Revolution,* p. 189.

Document 15. E. James Ferguson, *The Papers of Robert Morris, 1781-1784* (Pittsburgh, 1975), II, pp. 108-109.

Document 16. Marcus, *Jews and the American Revolution,* pp. 208-209.

Document 17. Marcus, *Jews and the American Revolution,* pp. 209-210.

Document 18. *Publications of the American Jewish Historical Society* 27 (1920), pp. 129-130.

Document 19. Marcus, *American Jewry. Documents. Eighteenth Century,* pp. 41-46.

Document 20. Edwin Wolf 2nd and Maxwell Whiteman, *The History of the Jews of Philadelphia* (Philadelphia, 1975 [1956]), p. 143.

Document 21. Marcus, *American Jewry Documents,* pp. 154-156.

Document 22. Marcus, *American Jewry Documents,* p. 47.

Document 23. Marcus, *American Jewry Documents,* pp. 51-52.

Document 24. Joseph L. Blau and Salo W. Baron, *The Jews of the United States, 1790-1840: A Documentary History* (New York, 1963), vol. I, p. 17.

Document 25. Marcus, *Jews and the American Revolution*, p. 124.

Document 26. Marcus, *Jews and the American Revolution*, pp. 213-216.

Document 27. Marcus, *Jews and the American Revolution*, pp. 219-220.

Document 28. William Addison Blakely, *American State Papers Bearing on Sunday Legislation* (New York, 1891), p. 40.

Document 29. Herbert J. Storing (ed.), *The Complete Anti-Federalist* (Chicago, 1981), vol. 4, p. 242.

Document 30. Marcus, *Jews and the American Revolution*, pp. 247-249.

Document 31. The United States Constitution.

Document 32. Marcus, *Jews and the American Revolution*, pp. 255-256.

Document 33. Marcus, *Jews and the American Revolution*, pp. 256-257.

Document 34. John Wingate Thornton, *The Pulpit of the American Revolution* (New York, 1970), p. 239.

Document 35. Margaret Wheeler Willard (ed.), *Letters on the American Revolution* (Boston, 1925), pp. 213-214.

Document 36. Oscar S. Straus, *The Origin of Republican Form of Government in the United States of America* (New York, 1885), frontispiece.

Document 37. *The American Republic and Ancient Israel* (New York, 1977).

Document 38. Conrad Cherry (ed.), *God's New Israel: Religious Interpretations of American Destiny* (Englewood, 1971), pp. 67-69.

Document 39. Thornton, *The Pulpit of the American Revolution*, pp. 400-403.

Document 40. *Publications of the American Jewish Historical Society* 27 (1920), pp. 34-37.

INDEX